W9-AJR-316

Beyond SCRAPBOOKS

QUARRY

First published in the United States of America by
Quarry Books, a member of
Quayside Publishing Group
33 Commercial Street
Gloucester, Massachusetts 01930-5089
Telephone: (978) 282-9590
Fax: (978) 283-2742
www.rockpub.com

Library of Congress Cataloging-in-Publication Data
Bourassa, Barbara C.
    Beyond scrapbooks : using your scrapbook supplies to make beautiful cards, gifts, books, journals, home decorations, and more! / Barbara C. Bourassa.
        p.   cm.
    ISBN 1-59253-229-2 (pbk.)
    1. Photograph albums. 2. Photographs–Conservation and restoration. 3. Scrapbooks. I. Title.
    TR465.B728 2006
    745.5—dc22   2005030584
                                                          CIP

ISBN 1-59253-229-2

10 9 8 7 6 5 4 3 2 1

Design: Susan Raymond
Cover: 12E Design
Photography by Allan Penn

Beyond SCRAPBOOKS

QUARRY BOOKS

Using Your Scrapbook Supplies to
Make Beautiful Cards, Gifts, Books, Journals,
Home Decorations, and more!

BARBARA BOURASSA

Contents

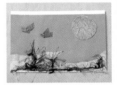

Chapter Three: Home Goods . . . 86

Introduction

Scrapbooking is one of the fastest growing crafts for women and girls—and with good reason. Who doesn't appreciate the beautiful books and pages that preserve our photos and mementos? But this popular pastime also has a wonderful silver lining: Using scrapbook materials, tools, and simple techniques, it's possible to make a wide variety of fun and unique paper crafts, cards, tags, and home decorations, such as embellished frames, customized calendars, and paper-wrapped candles.

It's as simple as using scraps of background papers to make a greeting card or as complex as binding a homemade book and decorating its spine with beads, charms, and ribbons. You can easily and quickly create an infinite number of beautiful and unique projects from scrapbook papers and vellums; embellishments such as ribbons, brads, and charms; as well as rub-ons; stickers; fiber; and more.

Consider, also, the many tools frequently used for scrapbooks, from rubber stamps and hole punches to scissors, decorative trimmers, and more. Combine these with the growing range of scrapbook techniques, and you'll quickly realize that the possibilities are endless.

When you build a scrapbook, mixed-media and collage techniques are encouraged—and so it goes with the projects featured here. A technique learned in one class, which applies to one project, can be recycled and reused for another project. A leftover snippet of ribbon, a paper scrap, or an incomplete box of grommets can find life in a new form. Even old pieces of jewelry, which I'm fond of collecting, can shine again as embellishments for cards, tags, and frames.

In the pages of this book you'll find some of my own creations as well as the work of many other talented designers and artists, both seasoned and new to the craft. And therein lies another beautiful aspect to the silver lining—you don't need to be a professional to create beautiful cards, tags, or home goods using scrapbook supplies, tools, and techniques—you just need your own imagination (and all that "stuff" you've been collecting).

—Barbara Bourassa

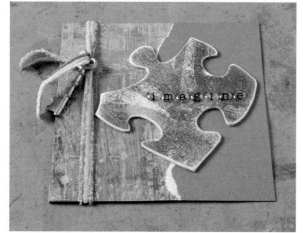

Getting Started: Tools and Techniques

WITH THE RISE IN POPULARITY of scrapbooking, the variety, design, and number of supplies available to artists has exploded. There are literally thousands of beautiful scrapbook supplies to choose from, and new items are released into stores every day. This fact, combined with the recent trend of mixed media, means no artist should ever be at a loss for creative inspiration.

What follows is a list of the basic supplies and tools available to artists. Depending on the store you visit, you may find fifty examples of each type of supply or just a handful. Although many large discount stores offer a good assortment of inexpensive scrapbook supplies, I also encourage you to visit specialty stores and websites for variation and inspiration. Other good places for supplies include garden and floral stores, hardware stores, art and graphic design suppliers, office-supply and stationery stores, large discount retailers, and sewing stores. Don't forget flea markets, yard sales, and thrift shops for truly one-of-a-kind finds, such as old jewelry, ephemera (e.g., maps, tickets, old photos), fabric, buttons, and the like. And never forget the great outdoors, where Mother Nature serves up an endless assortment of items such as feathers, shells, pebbles, sea glass, or twigs.

Paper

Paper is a central material in all of these projects—and the variety of beautiful patterned papers available right now is mind-boggling. Choices include decorative paper in hundreds of designs and themes as well as cardstock, vellum, tissue paper, and acetate. It's also increasingly easy to buy premade notecards, books, folders, tags, mats, and frames for easy decorating. And don't forget traditional photo supplies, such as photo corners or interesting photo papers.

Embellishments

This category is huge. And here's why: It includes everything from charms, brads, and eyelets to staples, clips, pins, fasteners, hinges, snaps, paper clips, buttons, tiles, zippers, ribbons, yarns, threads, and beads. The selection of alphabet letters is also growing, with new adhesive letters, stencils, and monogram letters appearing all the time. There are also a huge assortment of words and phrases available in such forms as metal plaques, rub-ons, fabric tapes, and vellum stickers. Speaking of stickers, choices include flat, three-dimensional, or clear quotes, phrases, photos, or illustrations to match any occasion or season.

Adhesives

Whether you're attaching a scrap of decorative paper or a piece of sea glass, every project requires some kind of glue. Choices here include glue lines and glue dots, foam squares, spray adhesive, glue stick, PVA glue, tape runners, or even a hot glue gun and glue sticks. When selecting adhesive, be sure to follow the manufacturer's recommendations—certain materials require special adhesives to create a secure bond.

Paint, Ink, and Markers

Acrylic paint is useful for any number of different projects. It's available at craft stores in a wide variety of colors, and it's not very expensive. Other choices in the paint and ink category include rubber-stamp inks, embossing powder, walnut ink, and a growing selection of markers, pens, gold-leafing pens, and the like. Applying paint may require a brush (although fingers work well, too); other choices include sponges, paintbrushes in a wide variety of sizes, or foam brushes.

Tools

All of these supplies are for naught, however, without the proper tools. Essential scrapbook tools include scissors, craft knife, cutting mat, bone folder, ruler, sandpaper, awl, hammer, and eyelet-setting tools. Corner rounders, blades, trimmers, deckle-edge scissors, wire cutters, flat-nose pliers, tweezers, drills, and brayers are also useful. You may also want rubber stamps or punches, of which there are thousands to choose from. And don't forget clamps, which can be useful when adhering larger or bulky pieces together.

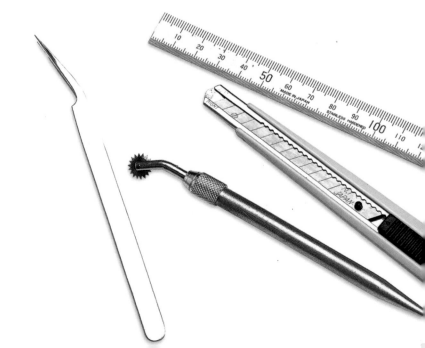

Chapter One: Cards and Tags

Scrapbooking is by definition a paper-based craft, and that fact is a wonderful benefit to anyone who makes cards and tags. First and foremost, there are hundreds of patterned papers, vellum, and cardstock to choose from, in all colors of the rainbow. Second, most of the embellishments that are designed for scrapbook pages can be attached to paper, which means they are perfectly suited for use on cards and tags. And third, because cards and tags are small by nature, they're quick and easy to make at home with just a few very basic supplies.

Attitude Is Everything **Card**

Designer: Amber Crosby

MATERIALS

- 8½" × 11" (21.5 × 28 cm) sheet of marigold cardstock
- 8½" × 11" (21.5 × 28 cm) sheet of raspberry cardstock
- one sheet of patterned paper
- "Attitude Is Everything" pre-made embellishment
- three assorted silk flowers
- 6" (15 cm) piece of ribbon
- seed beads

TOOLS

- cutting mat and craft knife
- glue
- scissors
- ruler

This bright and cheerful card is a snap to put together. The silk flowers add an elegant touch to the lower right-hand corner, but they would also work well in the center, positioned on the block of contrasting cardstock, or tucked into a die-cut vase or basket.

1. Cut a 5" × 7" (13 × 18 cm) card from the marigold cardstock using the ruler, cutting mat, and craft knife.

2. Cut a 4½" × 4½" (11.5 × 11.5 cm) piece from the patterned paper using the ruler, cutting mat, and craft knife.

3. Glue the patterned paper to the front of the card. Trim the ribbon to fit across the front of the card, and then glue it in place above the patterned paper.

4. Cut a 2" × 3½" (5 × 9 cm) piece of raspberry cardstock using the ruler, cutting mat, and craft knife. Glue in place on top of the ribbon, then adhere the "Attitude Is Everything" embellishment in the center of the cardstock.

5. Glue three flowers in the lower right-hand corner of the card. Add seed beads as embellishment.

Critter **Gift Cards and Tags**

Designer: Barbara Bourassa

Turtle Gift Card

MATERIALS

- 3" × 3" (7.5 × 7.5 cm) lavender gift card
- turtle charm
- small piece of bark
- blue, light turquoise, and purple glitter paint
- four small plastic flower beads
- three small green grommets
- one seed bead
- decorative sun brad
- ⅛" (0.3 cm) -wide sheer lavender ribbon
- decorative ribbon for the corner of the card

TOOLS

- glue
- scissors
- ⅛" (0.3 cm) hole punch
- paintbrush

These miniature critter cards combine animal charms with painted bark. You can find a wide range of charms and tiny animal figurines in craft stores, or use miniature fetishes, old pieces of jewelry, and bark chips or other found objects.

Turtle Gift Card

1. To decorate the bark: Paint an entire side of the bark chip with the light turquoise glitter paint. To create the pool, add a drop of blue glitter paint while the light turquoise paint is still wet, followed immediately by a drop of light turquoise paint in the pool. Let the paint dry completely.

2. Glue the grommets and the seed bead to the center of the flower beads and let dry. Glue the flowers to the edge of the pool, and then glue the turtle in place on the bark.

3. Punch a hole for the sun brad on the front of the card. To attach the sun with ribbon, loop the ribbon back and forth through the "spears" of the brad, then insert the brad into the card and secure on the back side by opening the spears.

4. Glue the decorated bark onto the front of the card. Punch a hole and add the ribbon.

Variation: Polar Bear Gift Card

To create this version, use dark blue paint on the bark, then add a drop of light green paint and a drop of lavender paint to create the moon. Glue the polar bear to the bark and adhere the bark to the tag.

Seashell **Gift Tag**

Designer: Barbara Bourassa

MATERIALS

- 2½" × 4" (6.5 × 10 cm) dark blue gift tag
- 2" × 3" (5 × 7.5 cm) light blue gift tag
- sea horse charm
- pink seed bead (to glue in place for sea horse eye)
- two small shells
- starfish charm
- decorative grommet
- assorted jewelry pieces
- green glitter paint
- clear glitter paint
- decorative sand-colored paper

TOOLS

- cutting mat and craft knife
- glue
- scissors
- ⅛" (0.3 cm) hole punch
- paintbrush
- computer and printer

1. Line up the tags on top of each other, then punch a hole in each tag using the ⅛" (0.3 cm) hole punch. Insert the grommet to secure the light blue tag on top of the dark blue tag. Add a drop of glue to the opposite end of the light blue tag.

2. Paint the seaweed using green glitter paint, then paint sand using the clear glitter paint. Glue the pink seed bead in place for the sea horse eye and let dry. Glue the sea horse to the tag. Glue the shells and starfish charm in place.

3. Typeset the "to" and "from" using a computer, then print the words on sand-colored paper. Trim the message to fit on the corner of the tag, then glue in place.

4. Re-assemble jewelry parts, beads, and other pieces to create a decorative "tail" for the gift tag.

I Love You **Card**

Designer: Carla Asmus

MATERIALS

- envelope template (below)
- one sheet of striped patterned paper
- one sheet of box of chocolates patterned paper
- one sheet of raspberry patterned paper
- 8½" × 11" (21.5 × 28 cm) sheet of cream cardstock
- heart bubblet sticker
- red thread
- pink thread
- pink sequins
- pink ribbon

TOOLS

- cutting mat and craft knife
- glue
- scissors
- ruler
- bone folder
- needle

This single-sided card combines two scrapbook papers with simple stitching. The miniature envelope on the front can be glued in place, as shown, used separately, or glued inside a folded card.

1. Cut a 7¼" × 6" (18.5 × 15 cm) piece of the striped paper using the ruler, cutting mat, and craft knife.

2. Cut a 4" × 6" (10 × 15 cm) piece of box of chocolates paper using the ruler, cutting mat, and craft knife.

3. Glue the papers together, then stitch them together using red thread.

4. Cut a 7¼" × 6" (18.5 × 15 cm) piece of the cream cardstock using the ruler, cutting mat, and craft knife. Glue the stitched papers onto the cardstock.

5. Enlarge the template provided, then cut out the envelope on the raspberry paper. Fold the triangular flaps toward the center, leaving the right triangle on top. Fold the flap to the back to close the bottom of the envelope. Cut a small piece of cream cardstock to fit inside the envelope. Embellish this small piece of cardstock with the heart bubblet sticker. Stitch along one edge using pink thread.

6. Tie a pink bow around the envelope and glue it in place on the front of the card.

7. To finish the card, glue on pink sequins along the top and bottom edges.

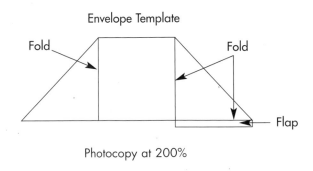

Envelope Template

Fold   Fold

Flap

Photocopy at 200%

Variation: Candy Wrapper

For a coordinated gift, personalize a candy wrapper! You can also use this technique to make decorative wine bottle labels or personalized labels for jam, nuts, or other homemade foods.

i love u · i love u · i love u · i love u · i love u · i love u · i love u ·

Dragonfly **Celebrate Card**

Designer: Sue Campbell

MATERIALS

- beaded metal dragonfly adornment
- white frosted paper
- 5" (13 cm) piece of thin-gauge wire
- 12" (30.5 cm) piece of textured yarn

TOOLS

- cutting mat and craft knife
- scissors
- ruler
- bone folder
- awl
- wire cutters
- computer and printer

This card was designed solely as a vehicle for using this beautiful beaded dragonfly embellishment. It sits on the edge of frosted white paper—which highlights the dragonfly's wire and beads—and appears ready to take off for the garden.

1. Typeset the "Celebrate" message on a computer and print along the right-hand side of the frosted paper.

2. Position the paper on the cutting mat and trim to 5" × 12" (13 × 30.5 cm). Measure and lightly score a line 3½" (9 cm) and 2½" (6.5 cm) from each short side.

3. Fold along each scored line toward the center of the card, where the edges of the card will meet. Make sure the edges close evenly, and then complete the folds using a bone folder.

4. Make a small hole with the awl and attach the dragonfly to the left-hand side of the card using a small piece of wire.

5. Attach textured yarn on the inside of the right-hand side of the card. To secure, tie a bow at the bottom of the card.

Celebrate **Wedding Card**

Designer: Lisa Grunewald

MATERIALS

- 8½" × 11" (21.5 × 28 cm) sheet of pink cardstock
- one sheet of embossed patterned paper
- 8½" × 11" (21.5 × 28 cm) sheet of vellum paper
- metal sticker
- metal "celebrate" word
- mini-brads
- pink ribbon

TOOLS

- cutting mat and craft knife
- glue
- scissors
- ruler
- computer and printer

This simple yet elegant wedding card is a one-of-a-kind gift that will be cherished for many years. For the inside, an Edwardian Script font is used to print the following message: May you always see each other through hearts filled with love.

1. Cut both the cardstock and the patterned paper to 7" × 11" (18 × 28 cm) dimensions using the ruler, cutting mat, and craft knife.

2. Fold one short edge of the patterned paper 2½" (6.5 cm) toward the center of the card. Fold the short edge of the patterned paper 2¾" (7 cm) toward the center of the card. Tear approximately ¼" (0.6 cm) off the edge of the first folded flap. When tearing, hold the printed side up and tear toward you to get the desired edge.

3. Fold the torn side to the center; the torn edge should overlap the cut edge just slightly.

4. Attach the metal sticker to the lower right-hand corner of the card, then add the "celebrate" word above it.

5. Line up the pink cardstock to the unprinted side of the patterned paper. Fold the cardstock to match the folds in the patterned paper, then tear the left-hand side to leave a small bit of pink showing under the patterned paper.

6. Print the card message on vellum and trim the vellum to 4¾" × 6¾" (12 × 17 cm).

7. Attach the vellum to the pink cardstock using two mini-brads.

8. Glue the pink cardstock inside the patterned paper. Tie the card closed with pink ribbon.

Japanese **Collage Card**

Designer: Sue Campbell

MATERIALS

- 5½" × 8½" (13.5 × 21.5 cm) white half-fold greeting card
- blue cardstock
- green craft paper
- yellow textured paper
- two multicolored brads
- assorted fiber, textured yarn, and ribbons

TOOLS

- cutting mat and craft knife
- ruler
- scissors
- glue

This card uses an assortment of brads, fiber, and ribbon to create a beautiful and unique collage. It has a Japanese look and feel, but you could alter this card easily for a Hawaiian, Latin American, or Chinese theme.

1. Measure and cut a piece of blue cardstock to fit the upper half of the greeting card. Glue it in place to form the "sky" on the top half of the card.

2. Cut two pieces of green paper into grass for the bottom of the card. Glue them in place along the bottom edge of the card.

3. Cut the fiber into 1" (2.5 cm) to 2" (5 cm) strands and glue on top of the green paper to serve as tall, wild weeds. Cut strands of the textured yarn and glue in place to serve as grass.

4. Cut a 1½" (4 cm) -diameter circle out of the yellow textured paper to make the sun, and then glue the sun in the upper right-hand corner of the card.

5. To make the butterflies, cut the fiber into 1" (2.5 cm) to 1½" (4 cm) pieces and attach them to the sky portion of the card using multicolored brads.

Wedding Gift **Card Enclosure**

Designer: Barbara Bourassa

MATERIALS

- gift card template (below)
- 8½" × 11" (21.5 × 28 cm) sheet of embossed white paper
- assorted wedding flowers, cake, and other embellishments or cutouts
- wedding photo banner stickers
- wedding word stickers (e.g., "soul mate," "together forever")
- miniature silver frame
- scrap paper for backing miniature frame
- 10" (25.5 cm) to 12" (30.5 cm) ¼" (0.6 cm) -wide sheer gold ribbon

TOOLS

- cutting mat and craft knife
- glue
- scissors
- deckle-edge scissors
- ruler
- bone folder
- pencil
- hole punch

This sweet and petite enclosure makes a more elegant outer covering for a gift card than the generic versions provided by stores. This enclosure is designed to hold a wedding gift card, but you could easily vary the materials to make it work for any number of occasions, such as graduation, birthday, teacher appreciation, or baby shower.

1. Enlarge and trace the template onto embossed paper, then cut out the shape using the ruler, cutting mat, and craft knife. Trim all the paper edges with deckle-edge scissors. (Alternatively, trace enclosure and then cut out using deckle-edge scissors.)

2. Score and fold the edges along the designated lines using the bone folder.

3. Punch holes as indicated on the template.

4. Decorate the exterior and the interior of the enclosure with embellishments and stickers. Back the miniature frame with scrap paper, and then attach the "soul mate" sticker in the center.

5. Fold the enclosure closed. Thread the ribbon through the holes, then thread the "I do" tag and "soul mate" frame through the ribbon and tie the ribbon closed.

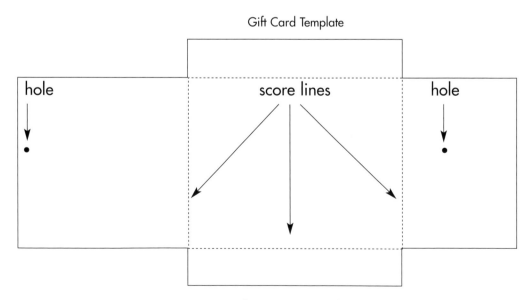

Gift Card Template

hole

score lines

hole

Photocopy at 200%

Thank-You **Card**

Designer: Carla Asmus

MATERIALS

- one sheet of blue damask patterned paper
- one sheet of English ivy patterned paper
- one sheet of textured green cardstock
- hydrangea border sticker
- flowers and gingham border sticker
- hummingbird bubblet sticker
- four eyelets
- 6" (15 cm) piece of ribbon

TOOLS

- cutting mat and craft knife
- glue
- scissors
- ruler
- bone folder
- eyelet hammer

This tri-fold card uses two different scrapbook papers and border stickers. The horizontal format could also be used for making a money holder.

1. Cut a 7 ½" × 9 ½" (19 × 24 cm) piece of green cardstock using the ruler, cutting mat, and craft knife.

2. Cut a 7 ¼" × 1 ½" (18.5 × 4 cm) piece of blue damask paper using the ruler, cutting mat, and craft knife.

3. Cut a 7 ¼" × 8" (18.5 × 20.5 cm) piece of English ivy paper using the ruler, cutting mat, and craft knife.

4. Tear the blue damask paper along the long edge. For the outside of the card, adhere the blue damask paper, then layer the English ivy paper over it and glue it in place.

5. Fold the two short edges into the center to make a tri-fold card. Cut a 7 ¼" × 3 ½" (18.5 × 9 cm) piece of English ivy paper and adhere it to the inside of the card.

6. Embellish the outside of the card with border stickers. Embellish the inside of the card with the hummingbird sticker.

7. Set two eyelets on the front side of the card. Pull ribbon through the eyelets and make a bow. Set two eyelets on the lower half of the card.

Paper Tissue **Flower Card**

Designer: Sue Campbell

MATERIALS

- 5½" × 4¼" (13.5 × 11 cm) matte notecard
- tissue paper scraps
- gold brads
- green textured paper
- textured yarn

TOOLS

- glue
- scissors

You can make this card in just minutes using scraps of tissue paper for the petals of the flowers and brads for the centers. To alter the design, substitute lightweight scrapbook paper, ribbon scraps, or fabric cuttings.

1. Tear a small strip of tissue paper and work it into a small flower-shaped design. Attach the flower to the notecard using a gold brad in the center. Continue making and attaching flowers to create a "flower bouquet."

2. Cut leaf stems out of the green textured paper, dab with glue, and insert behind the tissue paper flowers.

3. To create the grass, cut a 2" (5 cm) to 3" (7.5 cm) segment out of the green textured paper, apply glue to the back, and insert it beneath the flower bouquet at the bottom. Cut 2" (5 cm) to 4" (10 cm) strands of textured yarn and glue in place to create the three-dimensional grass on top of the textured grass.

I Miss You **Card**

Designer: Amber Crosby

MATERIALS

- 12" × 12" (30.5 × 30.5 cm) sheet of teal textured cardstock
- one sheet of patterned paper
- round tag
- fabric letter "i"
- silk flowers
- gingham ribbon
- teal mini-brad
- ink
- rub-on "you" word
- seed beads

TOOLS

- cutting mat and craft knife
- glue
- scissors
- ruler
- 2" (5 cm) square punch
- alphabet rubber stamps
- bone folder

This 6" × 6" (15 × 15 cm) card uses four different square blocks of patterned paper to convey its message. Each block could work alone, but the combination of four different bases for the different media makes an interesting and varied design.

1. Cut a 12" × 6" (30.5 × 15 cm) rectangle from the teal cardstock using the ruler, cutting mat, and craft knife. Fold into a 6" × 6" (15 × 15 cm) card and crease with bone folder.

2. Punch four squares out of the patterned paper. (Alternatively, cut out four squares measuring 2" × 2" [5 × 5 cm] using the ruler, cutting mat, and craft knife.) Glue the squares to the front of the card.

3. Glue the fabric letter "i" in the first square.

4. Stamp the word "miss" on the round tag. Attach a small scrap of ribbon to the top of the tag using the mini-brad. Glue the tag in the second square.

5. Place the "You" rub-on word in the third square.

6. Glue the three silk flowers in a triangle shape in the fourth square. Add the seed beads to the center of each flower.

Best Wishes **Wedding Card**

Designer: Debby Schuh for Anna Griffin, Inc.

MATERIALS

- one sheet of patterned vellum
- one sheet of patterned paper
- 8½" × 11" (21.5 × 28 cm) sheet of ivory cardstock
- flower die cut
- border sticker
- pink sheer ribbon
- foam squares
- sentiment tag
- envelope

TOOLS

- cutting mat and craft knife
- glue
- scissors
- ruler
- bone folder
- pencil

This elegant wedding card uses patterned paper and matching vellum—a trend you'll see more and more in scrapbook supplies—as well as a pleated border that adds an upscale touch.

1. Cut a 7" × 10" (18 × 25.5 cm) piece of the ivory cardstock using the ruler, cutting mat, and craft knife. Fold the cardstock in half to create a 5" × 7" (13 × 18 cm) card and crease with bone folder.

2. Cut the vellum to measure 7" × 9½" (18 × 24 cm) using the ruler, cutting mat, and craft knife. Glue the vellum to the outside of the card, starting on the back and wrapping around to the front. (The vellum should end approximately ½" (1.5 cm) from the right-hand edge of the card.)

3. To make the pleated border, cut three ½" x 12" (1.5 × 30.5 cm) strips of the patterned paper. Mark and score at ¼" (0.6 cm) and ½" (1.5 cm) intervals, alternating across the strips. Accordion fold each strip. Adhere all the strips to the right-hand edge of the card.

4. Cut the beaded edge from the border sticker and position it over the inner edge of the pleats.

5. Assemble the pieces of die-cut flowers with foam squares and adhere to the front of the card. Add the ribbon and sentiment tag.

6. Line the envelope with the patterned paper.

Imagine **Greeting Card**

Designer: Sandy Wisneski

MATERIALS

- 8½" × 11" (21.5 × 28 cm) sheet of cardstock
- one sheet of patterned paper
- self-stick letters (to spell "imagine")
- large puzzle piece from a child's puzzle
- textured ribbon
- key charm

TOOLS

- cutting mat and craft knife
- glue
- scissors
- ruler
- sanding block

Texture adds interest to a card and using a puzzle piece from a child's puzzle is the perfect addition.

1. Cut a 4½" × 9" (11.5 × 23 cm) piece of cardstock using the ruler, cutting mat, and craft knife. Fold the cardstock in half to form the 4½" × 4½" (11.5 × 11.5 cm) card.

2. Trim and tear the patterned paper to fit one side of the card, then glue in place.

3. Cover the large puzzle piece with glue, and then press the patterned paper onto the puzzle piece, rubbing along all the edges. Turn the puzzle piece over and cut around the puzzle shape using the craft knife.

4. Gently sand the edges of the puzzle piece with the sanding block. Be careful to sand downward in single swipes so as not to pull the paper away from the puzzle piece.

5. Attach the self-stick letters to the puzzle piece.

6. Wrap the ribbon around the card and tie the key charm into the knot. Trim the ribbon edges.

7. Glue the puzzle piece onto the front of the card.

Bamboo **Greeting Card**

Designer: Barbara Bourassa

MATERIALS

- 4¾" × 5½" (12 × 13.5 cm) yellow half-fold greeting card
- lime green vellum
- light blue vellum
- bamboo stickers
- 8" (20.5 cm) piece of variegated wire-edge ribbon

TOOLS

- cutting mat and craft knife
- glue
- ruler
- pencil

Jack, the subject of this photo, is adopted from Korea. His solemn face inspired this Asian-themed card that combines vellum, bamboo stickers, and variegated ribbon.

1. Cut a 4" × 4" (10 × 10 cm) block from the lime green and light blue vellum using the ruler, cutting mat, and craft knife. Position the lime green vellum on the front of the card and glue in place. Rotate the light blue vellum block to sit at an angle on top of the lime green block and glue in place.

2. Add the bamboo stickers along the sides of the card.

3. Curl the variegated ribbon around the pencil, and then adhere to the back of the photo. Attach the photo on top of the vellum.

Transparency Tulips **Greeting Card**

Designer: Sandy Wineski

MATERIALS

- one sheet of patterned paper
- 8½" × 11" (21.5 × 28 cm) sheet of transparency
- 8½" × 11" (21.5 × 28 cm) sheet of black cardstock
- 8½" × 11" (21.5 × 28 cm) sheet of tan cardstock
- ink pad
- black mini-brads

TOOLS

- cutting mat and craft knife
- glue
- tulip rubber stamp
- ⅛" (0.3 cm) hole punch

Overstamping on transparencies is an easy technique that produces endless combinations of cards. The colors in this background paper blend beautifully with the tulip silhouette.

1. Ink the rubber stamp using the ink pad.

2. Carefully stamp the image onto the clear transparency, trying not to rock the stamp image.

3. Set the transparency aside to dry completely. Allow five minutes for the ink to set.

4. Cut the decorative paper into a 4" × 4" (10 × 10 cm) square using the ruler, cutting mat, and craft knife. Cut this piece into four equal-size squares.

5. Cut the tan cardstock to measure 4⅛" × 4⅛" (10.5 × 10.5 cm) using the ruler, cutting mat, and craft knife. Glue the small squares of patterned paper onto the tan cardstock, leaving equal space around all the squares.

6. Cut the transparency to measure 4" × 4" (10 × 10 cm) using the ruler, cutting mat, and craft knife. Punch holes in four corners of the transparency and the tan cardstock, and then attach mini-brads through the transparency and the cardstock.

7. Trim the black cardstock to measure 4½" × 9" (11.5 × 23 cm) using the ruler, cutting mat, and craft knife, then fold in half.

8. Glue the tulip transparency onto the front of the card.

Chapter Two: Paper Crafts and Books

The paper-based nature of scrapbooking lends itself very well to the creation of books, albums, and journals. After all, making a book can be as simple as putting several greeting cards together for pages and adding a cover, although many of the projects in this chapter take that concept a few steps further. The wide assortment of beautiful decorative papers available for scrapbooking can also be used to make or embellish your own gift bags, calendars, or frames.

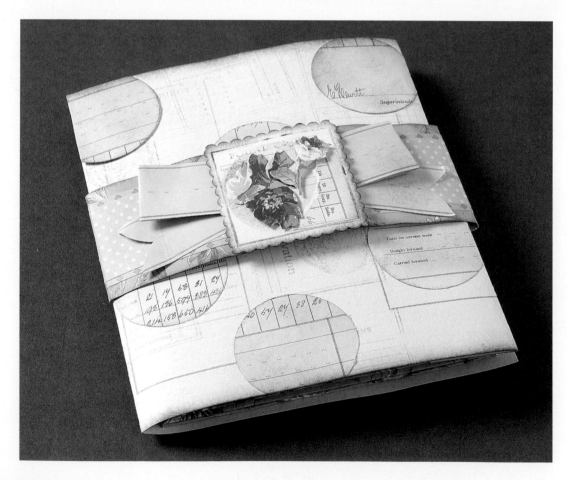

Altered Composition **Notebooks**

Designer: Sandy Wineski

Large Notebook

MATERIALS

- 7 ½" × 9 ⅝" (19 × 24.5 cm) composition notebook
- decorative paper
- die-cut tags with pre-existing holes
- fiber
- ink pad with three colors

TOOLS

- cutting mat and craft knife
- glue
- bone folder
- sanding block
- awl
- gesso
- cotton cloth
- paintbrush

You can create a quick and easy gift with this altered composition book. Be sure to select coordinating papers that can be overlapped for interest.

Large Notebook

1. Apply gesso to the spine of the notebook with a brush or your fingers, then let dry completely.

2. Using the edge of the ink pads, apply the three colors of ink to the spine. Blend the colors using a cotton cloth. Apply more ink as needed, then let dry completely.

3. Apply glue to the cover of the composition book. Place the paper onto the cover and rub flat. Be sure to rub along the edges and corners of the composition book to create a crease.

4. Fold the paper over the edges of the notebook, and then trim the excess paper along the edges. Trim a small "V" at the corners for a clean finish.

5. Apply glue to the paper being folded onto the inside cover and crease in place using a bone folder.

6. Cut another sheet of paper to fit on the inside of the notebook cover and glue it in place.

7. Tear a coordinating piece of paper to run horizontally across the cover, and then glue it in place.

8. Glue the two tags to the front of the cover so they are close but do not touch. Punch holes in the cover to match the holes in the tags.

9. Using several strands of fiber, weave them in and through the holes so that they tie in the center.

10. Finish the back cover of the notebook with coordinating paper.

Variation: Small Notebook

Follow the directions for the large notebook, then add a tag by punching a hole through the cover using an awl. Tie the tag using coordinating fibers.

Be **Embellished Journal**

Designer: Deborah Fay D'Onofrio

MATERIALS

- spiral-bound journal
- decorative scrapbook paper
- slide mount
- chopsticks
- black ribbon
- beige ribbon
- gold metallic acrylic paint
- pearl turquoise Lumiere paint
- black solvent ink
- white stencil paint
- gel medium

TOOLS

- cutting mat and craft knife
- glue
- scissors
- ruler
- bone folder
- pencil
- fine sandpaper
- paintbrushes
- garden nymph stamp
- lowercase alphabet stamps
- Asian-style stamps

You can make a unique gift in just minutes by embellishing a store-bought journal. The book shown here is spiral-bound, but any style of journal works well for this project. This book features an Asian theme for the decorations, but you can change the style of decoration to match any theme, such as horses for a teenage girl or gardening for someone with a green thumb.

1. Cut the chopsticks to the desired length using the cutting mat and craft knife. Sand the chopsticks with sandpaper. Wrap the chopsticks with the black and beige ribbons and glue them to the front of the journal.

2. Paint the slide mount with white stencil paint, then stamp the slide mount with the garden nymph stamp using black solvent ink. Accent with gold metallic paint.

3. Stamp the decorative scrapbook paper with lowercase alphabet stamps to spell "be." Paint a thin layer of pearl turquoise Lumiere paint over the paper to soften the look. Trim the paper to fit the back of the slide mount, attach it to the back of the slide mount, and then attach the slide mount to the cover with the gel medium.

4. Randomly stamp the inside pages of the journal with the Asian-style stamps.

reach within

Reach Within **Decorated Journal**

Designer: Deborah Fay D'Onofrio

MATERIALS

- perfect-bound journal with blank cover
- decorative scrapbook paper
- red textured fiber paper
- white cardstock
- ink-jet shrink plastic
- red, purple, and walnut ink
- black solvent ink
- Japanese sumi-e ink
- mini-brads
- clear embossing pad and powder
- soft gel medium

TOOLS

- scissors
- ruler
- bone folder
- trimming tool
- Asian-style stamps
- script stamp
- lowercase alphabet stamps
- embossing gun
- paintbrushes
- pencil
- toaster oven
- paper punch
- spray mister

This project is another beautiful example of how a store-bought journal can be customized with unique materials. This book is perfect-bound, but any style of binding can work.

1. Rip the decorative scrapbook paper and affix it to the cover and the spine of the book using the gel medium. Stamp the spine with both the Asian-style stamp (using black ink) and the script stamp (using red ink). Stamp the back cover with the Asian-style stamp and the text "reach within" in black ink.

2. Cut the white cardstock to the desired size for the art and text cover pieces. Spray them with the walnut ink, then let dry completely.

3. Stamp a small piece of the ink-jet shrink plastic with the Asian-style stamp using black solvent ink. Cut out the motif, punch a hole in the corner, and bake it in the toaster oven following the manufacturer's directions. Cool, then insert a mini-brad for decoration, and set aside.

4. Divide the piece into four sections with the sumi-e ink. Stamp one quarter with the script stamp using the red ink; in two quarters use a clear embossing pad and powder with Asian-style stamps and rub the final raised image with red ink; attach the finished shrink plastic embellishment to the last quarter with glue.

5. Rip the red textured fiber and glue it to the cover, then layer and glue both the cover art and the text to the red fiber.

Gift Tag Bag

Designer: Suzee Gallagher

MATERIALS

- five 2⅜" × 4¾" (6 × 12 cm) flat tags
- two 1½" × 3¼" (4 × 8 cm) single-fold gift tags
- acrylic paint
- ribbon
- 4⅝" × 3" (12 × 7.5 cm) muslin bag
- sequins
- beads
- cotton thread
- brown ink pad
- black ink pad

TOOLS

- glue
- scissors
- needle
- foam brush
- rubber stamps
- foam flower stamp

It's easy to turn extra scrapbook supplies—such as paper, tags, and scraps of ribbon—into unique and personalized gift tags and goodie bags. This project uses store-bought supplies that are decorated using paint, rubber stamps, and sequins.

1. Paint the tags as desired using the acrylic paint and the foam brush, then let dry completely. Distress the edges using black or brown ink pads.

2. Stamp the tags using the rubber and/or foam stamps.

3. Add assorted trims and ribbons, attaching the smaller single-fold tags into the ribbons.

4. For the matching gift bag: Paint the muslin bag using the acrylic paint. Let the paint dry completely.

5. Stamp the bag with the rubber and/or foam stamps to match the tags. Glue trim along the top edge. Stitch on the beads and the sequins as desired.

Fresh Flowers **Garden Books**

Designer: Christine Adolph

MATERIALS

- 12" × 12" (30.5 x 30.5 cm) sheet of transparency cut in half (6" × 12" [15 × 30.5 cm])
- two 6" × 12" (15 × 30.5 cm) sheets of patterned paper
- three or four 6" × 12" (15 × 30.5 cm) sheets of cardstock
- epoxy stickers
- two 20" (51 cm) pieces of sheer ribbon

TOOLS

- glue
- ruler
- bone folder
- ¼" (0.6 cm) hole punch

These simple and elegant journals, inspired by the colors of the garden, come together easily using just a few basic supplies. Although you end up with a book, there's no bookbinding involved. The pages use matching patterned and transparency papers, which create a beautiful layered look when adhered together.

1. Adhere two sheets of patterned paper, wrong sides together.

2. Fold the patterned paper from step one and the transparency sheet in half. Nest the patterned paper inside the transparency sheet to form a 6" × 6" (15 × 15 cm) book cover.

3. Punch a hole in the fold of the book cover approximately ¾" (2 cm) from the top, then punch a second hole ¾" (2 cm) from the bottom. Fold the cardstock in half to create the interior pages, and punch holes in the fold approximately ¾" (2 cm) from the top and ¾" (2 cm) from the bottom.

4. Nest the cardstock pages inside the book cover. Thread the ribbons through the punched holes and tie on the outside of the book.

5. To finish the book, add epoxy stickers to the front cover.

Josie Lynn **Baby Journal**

Designer: Stephanie McAtee

MATERIALS

- old book (inside pages will be removed)
- 4" × 6" (10 × 15 cm) mini-photo album
- patterned paper
- tags
- photo corners
- patterned tape
- chipboard alphabet
- acrylic paint
- words cut from book pages
- gesso
- ribbon
- brads
- silk flower heads

TOOLS

- cutting mat and craft knife
- glue
- scissors
- hole punch
- paintbrush

You can make this photo album in less than an hour, using an old book for the exterior and the pages from a mini-photo album for the interior. Embellish the journal with tags, ribbons, and collaged words.

1. Remove the inside pages of an old book using scissors or a craft knife, leaving the book cover intact. Remove the inner pages and photo sleeves of the mini-photo album.

2. Trim the patterned paper to size and adhere to the outside of the book. Place the photo sleeves on the inside of the book spine. Thread the silk flowers through the prongs of the brad before attaching the photo sleeves using the brads (the flower heads are visible along the spine of the book).

3. Apply gesso to the inside of book. Paint the chipboard letters. Embellish the inside of the book with patterned paper and painted chipboard letters.

4. To make tabs, cut small pieces of patterned tape. Glue cut-out words from book pages to the tabs. Adhere the tabs to the corresponding photo album page.

5. Adhere photo and photo corners to cover of book. Add title of the book.

6. To make a book closure, punch matching holes on the front and back covers. String ribbon through the holes, leaving excess to create a bow-tie closure.

Altered **Board Book**

Designer: Lori Roberts

MATERIALS

- 6¼" × 6¼" (16 × 16 cm) board book
- paper adhesive
- antique images
- trim and ribbon
- silk flowers
- silver star brads
- acrylic paint in assorted colors
- alphabet stickers
- typewriter alphabet stickers
- distress inks
- matte gel medium

TOOLS

- small foam brush
- foam stamps
- very fine sandpaper
- lint-free cloth or heavy-duty paper towels
- clean rubber brayer
- double-sided foam tape

This project takes an existing board book and builds on top of it. This way the binding and pages are already in place, and the heavyweight pages are durable enough to handle the adhesive and the weight of the added decorations.

1. Prep the board book by sanding all the pages. Use a damp cloth to wipe away any dust.

2. Apply the paper adhesive using the foam brush, and then adhere the decorative paper to each page, tearing to fit. Roll the rubber brayer over the pages to remove any air bubbles. Let the pages dry completely.

3. Apply two additional coats of paper adhesive, letting dry completely between coats. Trim any excess paper, and then sand the edges of the pages for a smooth finish.

4. Decorate the individual pages using trim, silk flowers, brads, images, acrylic paint, foam stamps, alphabet stickers, or other embellishments.

Embellished **Gift Bag**

Designer: Kitty Foster

MATERIALS

- 8" × 10½" (20.5 × 27 cm) brown paper gift bag
- one sheet of transparency
- three 12" × 12" (30.5 × 30.5 cm) sheets of decorative paper (one striped, one plaid, and one polka-dot)
- black ink
- ribbon scraps

TOOLS

- cutting mat and craft knife
- glue
- scissors

It's so easy to design a beautiful gift bag using scraps of decorative paper. This bag features a matching, removable tag that is held in place behind a sheet of transparency embellished with photocopied words.

1. Cut the polka-dot paper into a strip measuring 2⅝" × 7⅝" (7 × 19.5 cm) using the ruler, cutting mat, and craft knife.

2. Cut the striped paper into a strip measuring 2½" × 7⅝" (6.5 × 19.5 cm) using the ruler, cutting mat, and craft knife.

3. Cut the plaid paper into a strip measuring 4⅝" × 7⅝" (12 × 19.5 cm) using the ruler, cutting mat, and craft knife.

4. Ink the edges of all three papers to add depth. Let them dry completely, then glue to the bag with the polka-dot strip on the top, the plaid strip in the middle, and the striped strip at the bottom.

5. Photocopy birthday-related words onto the center of the transparency sheet. Trim the sheet of transparency to measure 4" × 5" (10 × 13 cm) using the ruler, cutting mat, and craft knife.

6. Cut four 2½" (6.5 cm) scraps of ribbon, fold each in half, and staple to the bag at each corner of the transparency.

7. Tie 5" (13 cm) scraps of ribbon to the handle.

Cupcake **Gift Card**

Designer: Kitty Foster

MATERIALS

- one 12" × 12" (30.5 × 30.5 cm) sheet of lime green cardstock
- four sheets of decorative patterned paper (one plain pink, one striped, one plaid, and one polka-dot)
- cupcake template (below)
- ribbon scraps
- black ink

TOOLS

- cutting mat and craft knife
- glue
- ⅛" (0.3 cm) hole punch

This sweet embellishment adds color and interest to the gift bag (project shown on page 57). You can also use the cupcake template to make a hanging tag; simply trace the cupcake onto cardstock, cut out and decorate, and attach it to the bag using a hole punch and a scrap of ribbon.

1. Cut cardstock into a piece measuring 10⅜" × 3" (26.5 cm × 7.5 cm) using the ruler, cutting mat, and craft knife. Fold in half to make the gift card.

2. Cut two small strips of plain pink paper and two small strips of plaid paper using the ruler, cutting mat, and craft knife. Ink the edges. Let dry completely, then glue in place at the top and bottom of the card.

3. Photocopy, and cut out the cupcake pattern. Trace the template onto the plaid and pink papers (pink for the icing and plaid for the cake). Ink the edges, then let dry completely. Glue the pieces together to make the cupcake.

4. Make sprinkles using tiny strips of paper and holes from the hole punch, then glue on top of the cupcake.

5. Cut a square from the pink paper measuring 2⅝" × 2⅞" (7 × 7.5 cm) using the ruler, cutting mat, and craft knife. Cut a second square from the striped paper measuring 2⅝" × 2⅜" (7 × 6 cm) using the ruler, cutting mat, and craft knife. Ink the edges, then let dry completely.

6. Glue the cupcake on the striped square, then glue the striped square to the pink square, and finally glue the pink square to the card.

7. Add a small hanging ribbon at the top of the card, and then insert the card behind the transparency pocket on the gift bag (see page 56).

Photocopy at 100%

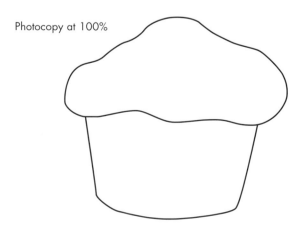

Belted **Brag Book**

Designer: Jeannine Stein

MATERIALS

- chipboard
- sandpaper
- decorative paper
- cardstock
- brads
- mini-brad
- buckle
- leather or ultrasuede
- beads
- waxed linen thread

TOOLS

- cutting mat and craft knife
- white glue
- ruler
- awl
- wire cutter
- bookbinding needle

This belted brag book resembles a designer purse with its leather trim and belted buckle wrap, yet it's quick and easy to make using chipboard for the covers and cardstock for the inside pages.

1. To make the book covers, cut two pieces of chipboard measuring 7¼" × 5¼" (18.5 × 13.5 cm) using the ruler, cutting mat, and craft knife. Round the corners of the cut chipboard with sandpaper.

2. Cut four pieces of decorative paper approximately ¼" (0.6 cm) bigger than the boards using the ruler, cutting mat, and craft knife. Glue one piece of paper to one side of the chipboard and trim it around the edges using the craft knife. Repeat the process on the remaining three sides of the book covers

3. Cut a piece of thin leather or ultrasuede measuring ¾" × 25" (2 × 63.5 cm). (It should fit around all four sides of the book with a small overlap.) Starting on one corner, brush white glue on the very edge of the book's cover and adhere the leather. Position the middle of the strip of leather right on the edge of the chipboard. Let dry. When dry, brush glue on one side of the leather and mold it to the cover, but do not glue completely in place. Tuck the corners in to fit.

4. Decide where to place the brads, and then make small holes using the awl. Push the brads through the holes and open the prongs on the other side. If the prongs are too long, trim them with a wire cutter. Glue down the other half of the leather to cover the prongs. Repeat this process for the second cover.

Continued

5. For the buckle, cut a piece of leather twice as wide as the buckle bar. It should be long enough to fit around the book and through the buckle. Brush glue in the middle of the piece of leather and fold the long sides into the middle. When dry, fold one end around the buckle bar and tack it in place with a mini-brad. Adhere the leather to the front of the book with brads. Cover the area on the inside of the front cover, where the brads appear, with a small circle of decorative paper.

6. For the inside pages, cut the cardstock to measure 6¾" by 12" (17 × 30.5 cm). Make an accordion fold, with the first fold ¾" (2 cm) from one edge, and subsequent folds 4¾" (12 cm) along. Repeat this process to make six pages in all. Overlap and glue pages together, leaving another ¾" (2 cm) fold at the end. Decorate the inside pages as desired.

7. Along each fold, measure 1" (2.5 cm) from the top and bottom edges and make a dot with a pencil. Use the awl (or paper piercer) to make a small hole at each dot.

8. Thread a bookbinding needle with about 36" (91.5 cm) of waxed linen thread. (Do not knot the end.) Enter hole #1 (see illustration A) from the valley side, leaving a 4" (10 cm) tail. Pick up a bead with the needle and enter hole #2 (see illustration B) from the mountain side. Push the accordion folds together with the bead in between. Enter hole #3 (see illustration C) from the valley side. Exit and add a bead, then enter hole #4. Continue this pattern until you reach the last fold. At the last fold, come back to the first fold using the same pattern of sewing, and then tie the ends of the thread together (see illustration D).

9. Glue the end flaps onto the front and back covers.

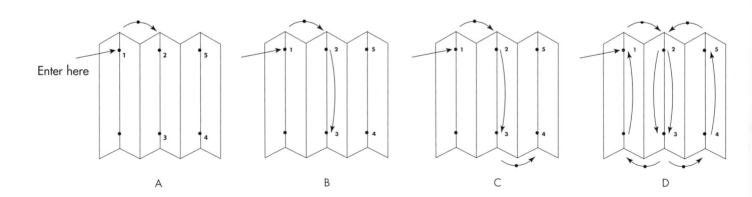

Enter here

A   B   C   D

A **Pocket** Full of Comfort

Designer: Deborah Fay D'Onofrio

MATERIALS

- shrink plastic (ink-jet-print-able for computer users)
- decorative scrapbook paper
- cardstock
- thin chipboard
- mesh
- thin wire
- miniglass vial
- heart charms
- embroidery floss
- waxed linen thread
- tissue scraps
- binding fibers
- acrylic paint
- solvent ink
- stamp ink
- pastels
- double-sided removable tape
- gel medium

TOOLS

- cutting mat and craft knife
- glue
- PVA glue
- scissors
- ruler
- bone folder
- pencil
- paper punch
- paintbrushes
- tweezers
- medium sandpaper
- lowercase alphabet stamps
- flower stamp
- toaster oven
- computer and printer

Each page of this mini-pocket book contains an inspirational quote with a theme such as "courage" and a shrink plastic pocket charm stamped with the sentiment. The charms can be pocketed as encouragement for the day.

1. Cut the chipboard to the desired size of the book. Cut the pages from the cardstock to match, using the ruler, cutting mat, and craft knife. Cover both sides of the chipboard with the decorative paper. Punch holes in the cover and the pages for binding later. Measure approximately ½" (1.5 cm) from the edges of the cover and the pages and score for easy opening and turning. On a computer, typeset and print the chosen quotes and cover text.

2. Cut the mesh and affix it to the cover. Position and adhere the title text on top. On a small scrap of paper, stamp "comfort" with ink, let dry, and affix. On another scrap, stamp the word "comfort". Wrap wire around the neck of the vial and attach the heart charm. Cut the second "comfort" into individual letters and tuck the letters into the vial. Make a stopper using a small piece of scrap tissue, then glue the vial to the cover.

3. Randomly stamp the book's pages with the flower stamp using acrylic paint. Tear out the printed quotes and decorate the edges with acrylic paint. Glue the decorative scrapbook paper onto the stamped cardstock. Cut the mesh to the desired size and adhere on three sides; leave the top open to create the "pocket." Stamp assorted sentiments on scrap paper and glue to the mesh pocket. Position a strip of double-sided tape inside each pocket to hold the charms in place.

4. Measure and cut the shrink plastic to roughly two times the size of the charms. Rough the surface gently using the sandpaper, then apply pastels and stamp sentiment using solvent-based ink. Punch a hole in each charm. Follow the manufacturer's instructions to shrink the charms. When the charms are complete, tie a small piece of embroidery floss and a heart charm through the hole in each charm.

6. Tuck the shrink-plastic charms into the pockets. Position the pages in the book. Apply glue on the inside of the front cover and wrap the fibers around the cover; end by tying the fibers in front. Bind the book using the waxed linen thread.

Hogan's **Papers**

Designer: Stephanie McAtee

MATERIALS

- mini-photo flip sleeves
- metal poetry tags
- bead chain
- acrylic paint
- magnetic alphabet letters
- staples
- patterned scrapbook paper
- book text
- plain file-folder file tabs

TOOLS

- cutting mat and craft knife
- diamond glaze adhesive
- hole punch
- paintbrushes
- sandpaper

This decorative memory file was created for the designer's dog, Hogan. It's made from an inner office envelope and a plastic sleeve that holds a miniature photo book. The file contains his pedigree papers and the mini-book is filled with photos from his first week in their home.

1. Cut the file folder in half. Seal the open end closed with adhesive, but leave the end with the flap and closure open for access to the papers and photos inside.

2. Attach file tabs at random points on the folder.

3. Attach a self-adhesive sleeve (which holds the mini-book of photos) on the folder's opposite side.

4. To make the miniature book, fold a piece of cardboard in half and adhere the mini-photo flip sleeves inside.

5. Cut the photos to size and place in the mini-photo book. Embellish the mini-photo book with metal tags, acrylic paint, the dog breeder's business card, and file tabs that identify the photos.

6. Attach the mini-photo book to a file tab by placing a hole in the tab then running bead chain through the tab and the mini-photo book. Distress the patterned paper using sandpaper.

SUNDAY DIMANCHE SONNTAG	MONDAY LUNDI MONTAG	TUESDAY MARDI DIENSTAG	WEDNESDAY MERCREDI MITTWOCH	THURSDAY JEUDI DONNERSTAG	FRIDAY VENDREDI FREITAG	SATURDAY SAMEDI SAMSTAG

January
THE MONTH OF *New Beginnings*

DECEMBER
S M T W T F S
          1 2 3 4
5 6 7 8 9 10 11
12 13 14 15 16 17 18
19 20 21 22 23 24 25
26 27 28 29 30 31

FEBRUARY
S M T W T F S
      1 2 3 4 5
6 7 8 9 10 11 12
13 14 15 16 17 18 19
20 21 22 23 24 25 26
27 28

						1
						New Year's Day Jour de l'An Neujahrstag
2	3	4	5	6	7	8
Epiphany Épiphanie	New Year's Day Bank Holiday in lieu of 1ˢ (U.K.)	Bank Holiday in lieu of 2ⁿ (Scotland)		Epiphany (traditional) Heilige Drei Könige		
9	10	11	12	13	14	15
16	17	18	19	20	21	22
	Martin Luther King, Jr. Day (U.S.)			Inauguration Day (U.S.)		
23 30	24 31	25	26	27	28	29

Garden **Calendar**

Designer: Barbara Bourassa

MATERIALS

- twelve 8½" × 11" (21.5 × 28 cm) sheets of colored paper (one for each month)
- twelve 4" × 6" (10 × 15 cm) photos of flowers
- 5½" × 7" (13.5 × 18 cm) twelve-month calendar
- garden and flower stickers
- grommets
- 15" (38 cm) of textured yarn
- 12" (30.5 cm) curved branch for hanging pages

TOOLS

- cutting mat and craft knife
- glue
- corner rounder
- hammer
- computer and printer

The inspiration for this calendar came from a collection of flower photographs. It's simple enough to make the calendar pages using craft paper, cut-up pages from a 5" × 7" (13 × 18 cm) calendar, and your own photos. Suspend the pages from a curved branch to continue the garden theme. Typeset the months using a computer and printer, or use month stickers instead.

1. Cut apart the calendar into twelve separate months and round all the corners. Round the corners on all the photos.

2. Adhere each flower photo and its matching month to a separate sheet of craft paper. Leave enough room at the top of each calendar page for punching the hanging holes.

3. Typeset each month name on the computer, then print out, trim, and glue in place on each corresponding page of the calendar.

4. Decorate the pages of the calendar using stickers.

5. Punch holes for hanging in the top of each page. Attach grommets to the holes. Thread textured yarn through each page and then loop over the branch to hang.

Cigar Box **Book**

Designer: Jenna Beegle

MATERIALS

- cigar box or blank wooden box
- blue craft paint
- green craft paint
- crackle medium
- rub-on letters
- chipboard letters
- lettering templates
- epoxy stickers
- watercolor crayons
- decorative paper
- cardstock
- ribbon
- bulldog clip

TOOLS

- glue
- scissors
- needle
- hole punch
- foam brushes
- foam alphabet stamps
- rubber stamps
- computer and printer

This treasure box book starts with a blank wooden box. Use an assortment of alphabet stamps, rub-on letters, and letters cut from chipboard to spell out inspirational words, such as "dream," "create," and "laugh." The miniature books inside feature inspirational quotes to match each theme.

For the Box

1. Base coat the box with several coats of green paint. Let dry completely.

2. Apply a thick coat of crackle medium to the box. Brush the medium on in one direction only. Let dry completely.

3. Apply a thin coat of blue paint to the box. Let dry completely.

4. Cover the box with a variety of inspirational words using the rubber and foam stamps with paint. Paint the chipboard letters, let dry, and then adhere them to the surface. Apply the rub-on letters. Trace the template letters onto the cardstock, cut them out, and adhere them to the box. Add the epoxy stickers.

5. Line the lid with cardstock. Use the rub-on letters to spell "Be You."

6. Color a piece of blank paper with the watercolor crayons. Rub a wet paintbrush over the colored areas to blend the colors. Let dry, then cut out a square to mat the white cardstock. Adhere the cardstock and mat to the inside lid.

7. To make a false bottom, cut a piece of foam core to fit the bottom. Cover it with decorative paper and use the letter stamps and paint to add a message. Use the smaller pieces of foam core to prop the covered piece up and glue them all in place. Decorate the false bottom with the letters as desired.

Variation: Inspirational Books

You can make a set of matching books for the inside of this box using cardstock, watercolor crayons, and ribbon.

Teacher's **Thank-You Book**

Designer: Deborah Fay D'Onofrio

MATERIALS

- decorative scrapbook paper
- cardstock
- ribbon
- chipboard
- black pen
- solvent ink
- stamp ink
- water-soluble oil pastels
- copper tape
- ephemera
- book ring binders
- gel medium

TOOLS

- cutting mat and craft knife
- scissors
- ruler
- bone folder
- pencil
- paintbrushes
- lowercase alphabet stamps
- compass/map stamp
- drill

This simple four-page book is designed as a thank-you gift for a teacher. The text inside reads as follows: A teacher helps us to chart our course for the future. She teaches us to navigate by finding our own North Star. We learn to believe in ourselves. She teaches us when to drop anchor and when to change course. We learn wisdom. She teaches us to sail for distant horizons. We learn inspiration. She teaches us there are no limits to the journeys we may take. We learn we are unlimited. And to our teacher we are grateful.

1. Cut the chipboard as desired to make two pages and two covers. Cover both sides of all the chipboard pieces with the decorative paper. Blend in oil pastels over each page as desired.

2. Stamp the pages with the compass/map stamp. Use stickers, letter ephemera cutouts, stamps, and the black pen to create your message. Affix all items using gel medium, then coat each page with gel medium to seal. Let dry completely.

3. Drill holes through the pages and covers, then seal the holes with the copper tape. Assemble the pages in order, pull through the book ring binders, and tie ribbons on the rings.

Stationery **Folio** and Handmade **Cards**

Designer: Jenn Mason

MATERIALS
- template (page 77)
- cardstock
- decorative paper
- color copy or original vintage ledger sheet
- vellum
- floral die cuts
- rubber-stamp ink

TOOLS
- cutting mat and craft knife
- glue stick
- decorative edge scissors
- ruler
- bone folder
- foam tape
- adhesive machine
- pencil
- paper clips
- markers
- hole punch
- die cutter
- circle punch
- rubber stamp

This beautiful stationery folio holds four handmade cards in an accordion-style pocket. For a simpler version of this project, skip the accordion pocket, tuck the cards inside the folio, and tie closed with a matching ribbon.

1. To create the folio: cut a cardstock folder to measure 6¼" × 12" (16 × 30.5 cm) using the ruler, cutting mat, and craft knife. Score two lines parallel to the shorter side; one should measure 1¼" (3 cm) from the left-hand edge and one should measure 6⅝" (17 cm) from the left-hand edge. Fold in along both of these score lines to create the folder with a 1¼" (3 cm) front edge flap on the inside.

2. Stamp the cover. Lightly cover photocopy of vintage ledger sheet with ink and punch out six circles. Adhere the circles to the cover and trim off the overhang. Lightly rub ink on the top and bottom of the folio.

3. To create the pocket accordion: Cut a 12" × 12" (30.5 × 30.5 cm) sheet of decorative paper in half diagonally in both directions, creating four triangles. (If desired, ink and stamp the unprinted side of one of the triangles for the first pocket.) Alternatively, trace and cut out four triangles using the template.

4. For all four pockets: Place the long side of the triangle at the top—this is the "top edge"—with the back side of the paper facing up. Measure in 3⅝" (9 cm) from each side along the top edge and make a small mark with a pencil. Fold the two side corners in with the fold at these marked points (see photo A, page 77). (The folds should be perpendicular to the top edge.) Fold the bottom corner up so that it just touches the top edge (see photo B, page 77).

5. For the three back pockets, glue the overlaps on the triangle to create the pockets.

Continued

6. For the front pocket: Fold the top corner down approximately 1¼" (3 cm) so that the fold lands where the two side flaps intersect (see photo C). Take the top side flap and fold it down so that the corner points to the bottom of the pocket and the top edge of that flap is now parallel with the side of the pocket. Repeat with the other side (see photo D). Tuck the corners under the front flap (see photo E) and secure the overlapping areas with glue.

7. Starting with the front pocket, use a small amount of glue to adhere the center of the back onto the next pocket. Repeat with all the pockets.

For the Cards

1. Cut four pieces of cardstock to measure 5½" x 8½" (13.5 x 21.5 cm) using the ruler, cutting mat, and craft knife. Fold each piece in half to create four 4¼" x 5½" (11 x 13.5 cm) cards.

2. Cut four strips of decorative paper to measure 1½" x 5½" (4 x 13.5 cm), then trim the long sides with decorative-edge scissors. Glue this paper on the inside of the card with the decorative edge toward the fold. Turn the card over and score a line 1" (2.5 cm) from the right-hand edge. Fold the paper back on this fold to reveal the decorative paper on the outside of the card. Add a torn piece of decorative paper under the flap.

3. Use a hole punch to punch the holes for the ribbon 2½" (6.5 cm) from the top edge. Punch one hole in the right-hand fold, one in the center fold, one in the back half of the card ¼" (0.6 cm) from the center fold, and one in the back half of the card ¼" (0.6 cm) to the right of the top right-hand fold

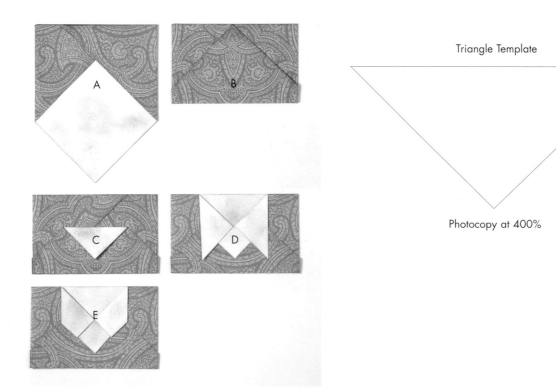

Triangle Template

Photocopy at 400%

4. Punch a tag and decorate with die cuts, marker, and ink. Thread 18" (46 cm) of ribbon through the tag, then through the hole in the front right-hand fold, then into the card through the hole in the center fold, back out through the next hole, and back up to the front through the last hole. Glue the top flap down.

5. Stamp a label on cardstock and cut out the label using decorative-edge scissors. Punch a mask with a circle punch and use a sponge to add a circle to the label. Tear a small piece of the vintage ledger paper and glue it on the label. Use foam tape to adhere the label and glue the tag onto the label. Tie the card shut and trim the ribbon ends.

Variation: For extra pizzazz, line the envelopes with coordinating paper, create a band to slide over the folio, or add extra vellum pockets to the interior to hold custom seals.

Child **Accordion Book**

Designer: Suzee Gallagher

MATERIALS

- 4¼" × 2" (11 × 5 cm) accordion fold tag booklet
- 4¾" × 3" (13 × 7.5 cm) muslin bag
- decorative patterned paper
- pink lowercase letters to spell "child"
- photo corners
- floral silver press-ons
- 35" (89 cm) piece of cream ribbon
- 8" (20.5 cm) piece of string
- beads
- dark pink ink pad

TOOLS

- cutting mat and craft knife
- glue
- scissors
- ⅛" (0.3 cm) hole punch
- "child" rubber stamp
- stapler and staples

This tiny book celebrates the innocence and gaiety of a child by mixing decorative paper scraps, bubble letters, press-on flower images, and stamped ribbon. Start with a store-bought accordion-fold tag booklet for quick execution.

1. Trim the paper to fit the upper 1½" (4 cm) of the tag booklet pages and then glue the paper in place on each tag.

2. Punch holes into each of the lowercase letters.

3. Add the photos and the photo corners to each tag. Fold the string in half, add beads to the end, and secure under one of the photos.

4. Ink the sides of each tag using the dark pink ink pad.

5. Add the floral silver press-ons as desired.

6. Stamp the "child" rubber stamp along the length of ribbon, and then trim into 7" (18 cm) pieces to fit each tag.

7. Thread each 7" (18 cm) section of ribbon through the hole at the top of the tag, and then attach each pink lowercase letter using a staple. Repeat to spell out "child" across all five tags.

8. For the matching bag, add the floral silver press-on to the front, then stamp the "child" rubber stamp above and below the silver image.

Hawaiian **Dos-a-Dos** Book

Designer: Hollly Sar Dye

MATERIALS

- one 12" × 12" (30.5 × 30.5 cm) sheet of sand-colored cardstock
- two 12" × 12" (30.5 × 30.5 cm) sheet of white cardstock
- 8½" × 11" (21.5 × 28 cm) sheet of blue cardstock
- 1½" × 3½" (4 × 9 cm) scrap of red cardstock
- beach stickers
- 12" (30.5 cm) red sewing floss or waxed linen thread
- two colors of brown rubber-stamp ink

TOOLS

- cutting mat and craft knife
- white glue
- ruler
- bone folder
- double-sided mounting tape
- needle
- small hibiscus rubber stamp
- large hibiscus rubber stamp

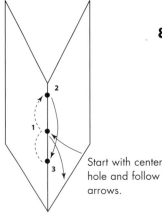

Start with center hole and follow arrows.

This simple little book comes together quickly and easily using several sheets of cardstock. Creating a Hawaiian theme is easy using two different size hibiscus rubber stamps.

1. Using the ruler, cutting mat, and craft knife, cut the sand cardstock to measure 4" × 12" (10 x 30.5 cm). Cut the white cardstock into four pieces measuring 7¾" × 3⅞" (20 × 10 cm) and, cut the blue cardstock to measure 8½" × 1" (21.5 × 2.5 cm).

2. Select a Hawaiian sticker and adhere it to the scrap piece of red cardstock. Cut the cardstock around the sticker, leaving a ⁷⁄₁₆" (1.5 mm) mat.

3. Fold the sand cardstock into thirds. The first fold from the left-hand side is an origami "valley fold." From the right-hand side, make a "mountain fold." Reinforce the folds using a bone folder.

4. Fold each of the four white pieces of cardstock in half. Nest one sheet inside a second sheet. Set this aside. Repeat with remaining two sheets.

5. Rubber-stamp the front cover of the sand-colored cardstock using the two colors of ink and the two rubber stamps. Repeat on the other cover.

6. Slide the first pair of white pages between the front and back cover. Using a ruler, locate the center point of this book. Locate and mark a point to the left and to the right of the center point; they should be equal distance from the center point.

7. Using a sewing needle, poke three holes through the entire book. Bind the book using a pamphlet stitch (see illustration, left). Flip the book over and repeat steps six and seven.

8. Gently wrap the blue strip of cardstock around the closed book. Lightly mark where you will fold and score the blue piece (about ⅛" [0.3 cm] on the left-hand spine, same on the right-hand side). After the folding and scoring, glue one end of the blue strip down. Affix the matted Hawaiian sticker with double-sided mounting tape to the center of the blue strip, hiding the spot where glue was applied. Slip the blue band over the dos-a-dos book.

Sewn Paper **Gift Bags**

Designer: Suzee Gallagher

MATERIALS

- four 12" × 12" (30.5 × 30.5 cm) sheets of decorative patterned paper (two dark green, two contrasting light green)
- cotton thread
- two brown paper handles
- paper scraps for tags
- ribbon

TOOLS

- cutting mat and craft knife
- scissors
- sewing machine with straight stitch

If you have a sewing machine and decorative scrapbook paper, you can make your own gift bags. The beauty of this project is its scalability—you can make a large gift bag using four sheets of 12" × 12" (30.5 × 30.5 cm) scrapbook paper, or stitch up smaller versions using scraps and leftovers. The trick goes like this: The two side panels and the bottom should be half the size of the large sides. For a 12" × 12" (30.5 × 30.5 cm) bag, for instance, the large sides will measure 12" × 12" (30.5 × 30.5 cm), but the side panels and bottom will measure 6" × 12" (15 × 30.5 cm).

1. From the decorative paper, cut out the two side panels measuring 6" × 12" (15 × 30.5 cm) using the ruler, cutting mat, and craft knife. Cut out one piece for the bottom measuring 6" × 12" (15 × 30.5 cm) using the ruler, cutting mat, and knife.

2. Sew all four sides of the bag together, leaving ¼" (0.6 cm) at the bottom of each side. Sew the bottom of the gift bag to the sides.

3. Sew the handles to the inside of the bag.

4. To make the tag, stitch together scraps of contrasting paper, then tie it to the bag using the ribbon.

Variation: Striped Bag

For the striped version of the bag, follow the same directions but substitute two striped 12" × 12" (30.5 × 30.5 cm) sheets of paper, one contrasting polka-dot sheet, and one contrasting plaid sheet. Attach a monogram letter to the tags using the fiber, and then tie the tags to the bag.

Miniature **Slide Frame**

Designer: Sandy Wisneski

MATERIALS

- three photos measuring about 1½" × 1¾" (4 × 4.5 cm)
- one 12" × 12" (30.5 × 30.5 cm) sheet of pink patterned paper
- three 2" × 2" (5 × 5 cm) cardboard slide mounts
- ten ⅛" (0.3 cm) eyelets
- 12" (30.5 cm) of textured fiber
- two miniature metal charms

TOOLS

- cutting mat and craft knife
- glue
- ⅛" (0.3 cm) punch
- thin wire

Family pets hold a special place in our hearts. You can display that love proudly with this series of slide-mount frames.

1. Cut the cardboard slide mount along the crease line so that you are only using one side of the mount. (This is necessary because otherwise the cardboard is too thick to attach the eyelets.)

2. Cut three squares of paper measuring about ½" (1.5 cm) larger all around than the slide mount. To attach the patterned paper to each of the cardboard slide mounts, apply glue to the front of the slide mount, then press the paper firmly onto the glue. Crease along all the edges.

3. Turn the slide mount over and use the knife to cut an "X" in the center of the slide mount opening. Crease the paper from the inside of the opening. Glue it down onto the back of the slide mount. Trim any excess paper.

4. Crease the paper over the outside edges to the back. Cut a "V" at the corners to make a clean fold at the corners. Glue the paper to the back of the slide mount, trimming any excess paper. Let the glue dry completely.

5. Insert the photos behind each slide mount, and then back the slide with a small piece of patterned paper. Glue in place and let dry completely.

6. Punch holes in the slide mounts evenly along the top and bottom edges. The first two slides will have four holes each, while the last slide has only two holes. Attach the eyelets.

7. String the fiber through the eyelet holes, starting at the bottom slide mount. Bring each end up through the eyelet on each side. String both ends back down through the bottom eyelets, bringing the fiber back to the front of the slide mount when you are at the top holes. Continue this process through the last slide mount and tie a knot at the top.

8. Attach the charms to the top eyelet using a small piece of wire.

Chapter Three: Home Goods

Decorative scrap paper and supplies lend themselves beautifully to home goods such as frames, candles, trays, coasters, and other flat surfaces. But they can also be used on three-dimensional accessories—such as on a decorative door wreath—or to embellish a tin or dress up packaged soap.

COLORFUL

a faithful friend

g o o d   d o g

Decorative **Mirrors**

Designer: Linda Blinn

Hot Pink Mirror

MATERIALS

- 10" × 10" (25.5 × 25.5 cm) square wood-framed mirror
- 12" × 12" (30.5 × 30.5 cm) decorative patterned paper
- beads, dried flowers, yarn, beach glass, etc.
- one sheet of transparency
- rub-ons
- epoxy stickers
- vellum tape

TOOLS

- craft knife
- glue
- scissors
- low-tack painter's tape
- burnishing tool

Ocean Theme Mirror

MATERIALS

- 10" × 10" (25.5 × 25.5 cm) square wood-framed mirror
- two 12" × 12" (30.5 × 30.5 cm) sheets of decorative patterned paper
- 12" × 12" (30.5 × 30.5 cm) sheet of decorative map patterned paper
- stickers, dried flowers, postage stamps
- one sheet of transparency
- sea glass
- press-on alphabet letters
- vellum tape
- ink pads

These decorated mirrors may look difficult but in fact they come together quickly and easily due to their flat surface and perfect size—10" (25.5 cm) square, which is just right for a 12" × 12" (30.5 × 30.5 cm) piece of scrapbook paper.

Hot Pink Mirror

1. Cover the mirror surface with low-tack painter's tape to protect the mirror while attaching the papers. Apply glue to the back side of a 12" × 12" (30.5 × 30.5 cm) piece of scrapbook paper. Lay the mirror face down in the center of the glued surface, then turn the mirror over and burnish the paper on the front side to remove all the air bubbles. Bring the edges of the paper around the sides and adhere them to the back.

2. Cut an "X" in the center of the paper over the mirror. Trim sides to ½" (1.5 cm) and glue in place. Cut a section of a transparency to fit over the mirror, allowing at least a 1 ½" (4 cm) border.

3. Place embellishments inside the hollow space over the mirror and adhere the transparency on top using vellum tape.

4. Embellish the mirror using yarn, postage stamps, and small pieces of transparency.

Ocean Theme Mirror

1. Cover the mirror surface with low-tack painter's tape to protect the mirror while attaching the papers. Collage torn pieces of scrapbook paper and maps to the front of the mirror. Bring edges over the side of the wood frame. Adhere papers with glue and burnish to remove any air bubbles.

2. Use an ink pad to blend the papers and highlight the edges of the papers. Add stickers, dried flowers, and postage stamps as accents.

3. Remove the tape from the mirror. Adhere sea glass to the corner of the mirror using diamond glaze. Spell "sea" on the mirror using silver press-on alphabet letters.

4. To finish the mirror, glue a 10" × 10" (25.5 × 25.5 cm) piece of matching scrapbook paper to the back.

Springtime **Altered Box**

Designer: Wendy Morris

MATERIALS

- 4" × 6" (10 × 15 cm) unfinished wooden box
- brads
- silk flowers
- decorative scrapbook paper
- cardstock stickers
- metal word plaques
- fiber
- glass capsule
- ribbon
- stamping ink
- craft paint
- diamond glaze

TOOLS

- cutting mat and craft knife
- glue
- glue dots
- scissors
- ruler
- foam paintbrush
- cosmetic sponge
- stamps

This three-dimensional altered box opens to reveal four inspirational messages inside. For variety, use this technique to create a box featuring four miniature photos.

1. Paint the outside of the wooden box with acrylic paint. Let the paint dry completely. Cut two pieces of decorative paper to measure 4" × 6" (10 × 15 cm) using the ruler, cutting mat, and craft knife, and then adhere to the front and back of the box using glue.

2. Apply a frame sticker to the front of the box, followed by a smaller sticker. Attach a silk flower to the center of the large frame sticker using a glue dot. Pull the adhesive strip from the back of the "inspire" word charm and attach the charm to the center of the small square sticker. Cut the ribbon to 4" (10 cm) and attach it to the front of the box using glue.

3. Use a cosmetic sponge and acrylic paint to apply paint to the front of the "imagine" and "dream" word charms. Apply the paint to fill the grooves of the letters, and then lightly wipe away the excess paint from the charms.

4. Open the box and paint the windows inside the box with acrylic paint. Let the paint dry. Cut four 2" × 3" (5 × 7.5 cm) pieces of decorative paper to fit inside the four windows. Glue in place.

5. For the first window, adhere a picture of choice, then attach the "imagine" word charm. For the second window, attach a "believe" cardstock sticker. For the third window, attach a "dream" cardstock sticker, then the "dream" word charm. Attach a brad in the center of a silk flower and adhere the flower using a glue dot. For the fourth window, adhere a photo of choice, then punch out letters and adhere.

6. Cut the fiber to the desired length and tie it to the hinge closure of the box.

7. Stamp a phrase, definition, or quote on a scrap of paper. Cut the paper to fit inside the glass capsule. Roll the paper and slide it into the glass capsule. Adhere the ends of the glass capsule with diamond glaze and let dry completely. Finally, thread the fiber through one end of the glass capsule and tie the fiber.

Gerber Daisy **Coasters**

Designer: Michelle Hill

MATERIALS

- 8 ½" × 11" (21.5 × 28 cm) sheet of cardstock
- four tumble tiles
- tissue paper
- quote rub-ons (such as "treasure each day")
- gerber daisy clip art (one pink, one blue, one green, and one orange)
- pink adhesive felt

TOOLS

- water-based sealer (e.g., Mod Podge)
- scissors
- foam brush
- computer and printer

Tumble tiles can be found in your local hardware store in the tile section (they usually come in a pack of ten). These tiles make wonderful gifts. You can also print your family photos out on tissue paper and adhere them to the tiles to create a fun and festive gift for family members.

1. Adhere tissue paper to the front of the cardstock at the edges and corners. Place the tissue paper/cardstock in the printer tray. Print the four gerber daisy clip art images onto the tissue paper.

2. Carefully remove the tissue paper from the cardstock. Cut out the four daisy images and set them aside.

3. Apply water-based sealer to the top of the tile. Take each daisy image and lay it on top of the sealer. Press the image lightly onto the tile, using your fingertips to press out any wrinkles or bubbles.

4. Using a foam brush, apply several coats of water-based sealer over the image, letting the sealer dry completely in between coats.

5. Repeat the process with the three remaining tiles.

6. Apply the rub-on quotes to each tile.

7. Cut a piece of adhesive felt to match the bottom of the tile, and adhere using self-adhesive.

when

he

was

a

little boy

Little Boy **Frame**

Designer: Allison Strine

MATERIALS

- unfinished wooden frame
- decorative patterned paper
- clip art images or cut-up toy catalog
- water-soluble markers
- vintage motorcycle toy
- gel medium
- white paper
- rubber-stamp ink

TOOLS

- cutting mat and craft knife
- decoupage glue
- rubber stamps

This project, like many others in this book, starts with an unfinished wooden object, then adds color, images, and dimension using scrapbook paper, cut-out images, and a small toy on the top edge. To speed things up, you can also stamp the letters directly onto the frame using permanent ink. You won't be able to move the letters around, but it's quicker.

1. Use the decoupage glue to cover the blank frame with patterned paper. Trim any excess and let dry completely.

2. Use a craft knife to cut images from an old toy catalog. Stamp words onto plain white paper with ink. Apply three layers of gel medium to words and images, letting each layer dry before adding the next. Soak in water, then gently rub the paper away, leaving a transparent image. Color the images with markers, then adhere them to the frame using gel medium.

3. Glue a toy motorcycle on the top of the frame.

Garden **Votive Candleholder**

Designer: Barbara Bourassa

MATERIALS

- 3" × 2½" (7.5 cm × 6.5 cm) -wide glass votive candleholder
- picket fence paper cutouts
- dark green grass cutouts
- light green grass cutouts
- morning glories and other assorted flower cutouts
- watering can cutout
- small piece of transparent green paper (for bottom of candleholder)
- assorted votive candles

TOOLS

- glue
- scissors

This votive candleholder is based on an English cottage garden theme, with a white picket fence and morning glories, but you could change the materials to reflect your own garden, the season, or a special occasion. Using a square votive candleholder makes it easy to attach the paper cutouts to a flat surface, but a round candleholder will also work.

1. Trim a small piece of transparent green paper to fit the outside of the candleholder and glue in place.

2. Glue the grass cutouts in place, followed by the picket fences. Attach the flowers in a decorative fashion, weaving the stems into the fence and trimming off flowers, leaves, or stems as needed.

3. Trim the edges of the fence to match or abut neatly at the corners. Cover any rough edges or open spaces with additional flowers and leaves. Add a watering can or any final accents as desired.

Stamped **Soap** and Matching **Bag**

Designer: Suzee Gallagher

MATERIALS

- 2½" × 4½" (6.5 × 11.5 cm) muslin bag
- unwrapped soap to fit in bag
- small scrap of transparency
- plastic wrap
- magenta ink pad
- black ink

TOOLS

- scissors
- permanent markers
- flower image rubber stamp
- diamond shape rubber stamp

This sweet little project makes a perfect hostess gift or a quick and easy party favor.

1. Using the magenta ink pad and black ink, stamp the flower image onto the muslin bag. Color in the images using the permanent markers.

2. For the center decal on the bag, stamp the flower design onto a scrap of transparency and color in the design. Trim the transparency to fit the bag, and then glue it to the outside of the bag using a small dot of glue.

3. For the soap, stamp the diamond image onto a small piece of transparency, then color in the image using permanent markers.

4. Adhere the image to the unwrapped soap using a small dot of glue, then wrap the soap in plastic wrap and slip it into the matching bag.

Altered **Child's Tin**

Designer: Kitty Foster

MATERIALS

- 4½" × 10" (11.5 × 25.5 cm) metal tin
- spray-on metal paint in pink and orange
- lime green paint pen
- ribbon
- decorative patterned paper
- 6¼" × 2¾" (16 × 7 cm) matching sticker
- ink pad

TOOLS

- glue dots
- sandpaper
- screwdriver

This easy project starts with an inexpensive metal tin and then adds decorative paper, ribbon, and assorted embellishments to dress it up. You can use these same techniques and ideas on a wastebasket, pencil holder, birdhouse, watering can, or any other indoor-use metal object.

1. Spray paint the tin with the pink spray paint and let it dry completely.

2. Spray paint the tin with the orange paint and let it dry completely.

3. Using the sandpaper, sand down the orange paint to let the pink paint show through. Use the screwdriver to "ding" up the orange paint to let the pink paint show through.

4. Use the lime green paint pen to paint the top edges of the tin.

5. Trim the ribbons and attach them to the handles of the tin.

6. Trim a strip of paper approximately 2" (5 cm) wide to fit around the tin. Ink the edges to add depth, then let dry completely. Adhere it onto the tin using the glue dots.

7. Cut two sections of ribbon to fit around the tin, then glue in place, one on top of the other, on the decorative paper.

8. Ink the edges of the large sticker, then place in the center of the tin, on top of the decorative paper and ribbons.

Seaside **Altered CD**

Designer: Sarah Tyler

MATERIALS

- beach-tag stickers
- decorative patterned paper
- blue organza ribbon
- assorted fibers
- blue flat marbles
- miniature gold eyelets
- CD
- gold spray paint

TOOLS

- hot glue gun and glue sticks
- dimensional adhesive
- scissors
- water-based sealer (e.g., Mod Podge)
- hole punch

Here's a fun and innovative way to turn an old CD into a piece of artwork. This disc features an ocean theme, but you can easily substitute flowers, pets, or tropical fish for a different look and feel.

1. Spray paint the CD using the gold paint.

2. Tear strips of decorative papers and adhere them to the CD using the water-based sealer. Embellish the CD with the stickers.

3. Use the dimensional adhesive to enhance the stickers and the torn edges of the paper. Adhere glass marbles and fiber accents using the dimensional adhesive.

4. Stick the matching tag stickers back-to-back. Trim the edges. Set the tags with a gold eyelet. Add the dimensional adhesive to the tag stickers, letting one side dry before applying to the other side.

5. Thread the tags with ribbon and fibers. Adhere to the back of the CD using hot glue. Make a loop of ribbon and fibers for the hanger and adhere with the hot glue.

Dela Tribute **Frame**

Designer: Barbara Bourassa

MATERIALS

- 5" × 5" (13 × 13 cm) unfinished wooden frame
- two 12" × 12" (30.5 × 30.5 cm) sheets of patterned paper
- metal word plaque ("a faithful friend")
- 12" (30.5 cm) piece of sheer ribbon
- small plastic dog bone
- bubble alphabet letters
- alphabet letter tags
- watercolor paints

TOOLS

- glue
- water-based sealer (Mod Podge)
- paintbrush

This frame serves as a tribute to Dela, the coonhound shown in the photo. To create this frame, torn strips of decorative paper were adhered to a simple wooden frame using water-based sealer, and then the surface was tinted using watercolor paint. The embellishments include a metal word plaque, Dela's name spelled in alphabet tags, and a small dog bone tied on with a sheer lavender ribbon.

1. Tear strips of the patterned paper and adhere them to the frame using the water-based sealer. Let dry completely, then add additional pieces as needed to cover the surface of the frame. Let the frame dry completely.

2. Using the paintbrush, tint the surface of the frame using the blue, purple, and green watercolor paints. Let the frame dry completely.

3. Add the word plaque and the bubble alphabet letters using the adhesive on the back of each. Tie on the small bone using a 4" (10 cm) piece of sheer ribbon. Loop a second piece of sheer ribbon through each alphabet letter tag to spell the dog's name, and then adhere to the corner of the frame.

DELIA

a faithful friend

good dog

Altered "C" Letter

Designer: Dana Smith

MATERIALS

- unfinished wooden letter "C"
- silk flowers
- decorative patterned paper
- solid-colored cardstock
- brads
- ribbon
- craft paint

TOOLS

- glue
- scissors
- paintbrush
- pencil
- $1\frac{1}{2}$" (4 cm) circle punch
- $\frac{1}{4}$" (0.6 cm) hole punch
- computer and printer

This altered letter makes a beautiful decoration for a young girl's room or bulletin board. You can also use altered letters to spell out a message, such as "Joy," or to spell a pet's name above his food and water bowls.

1. Lightly dry-brush pink and white craft paint over the wooden letter, allowing plenty of wood to show through.

2. Lay the wooden letter upside down on the back of a sheet of scrapbook paper and trace the letter. Cut out the letter and adhere it to the front of the wooden letter.

3. Remove the center of the silk flowers and lightly brush pink paint over the flowers. Secure a brad in the center of the flower and adhere the flower to the letter.

4. Print the child's name on a piece of solid-colored cardstock. Punch out the name with $1\frac{1}{2}$" (4 cm) circle punch. Use a $\frac{1}{4}$" (0.6 cm) hole punch to punch a hole at the top of the circle. Fill the hole with a brad, and then attach the name to the letter.

5. Tie ribbons on the top and the bottom of the wooden letter.

Altered **Gift Can**

Designer: Carla Asmus

MATERIALS

- cardboard and tin gift can
- one 12" × 12" (30.5 × 30.5 cm) sheet of wild rose patterned paper
- one 12" × 12" (30.5 × 30.5 cm) sheet of green-striped paper
- cream cardstock
- flower border sticker
- vine border sticker
- gingham border sticker
- rose bubblet sticker
- pink ribbon
- artificial pink rose

TOOLS

- cutting mat and craft knife
- glue
- hot glue gun and sticks
- ruler

What better way to wrap a uniquely shaped gift than to use an altered gift can? Once the gift has been unwrapped, the can is beautiful enough to use on a dresser or shelf for storage.

1. Cut coordinating patterned papers to fit on the top and the bottom halves of the can using the ruler, cutting mat, and craft knife. Glue the papers in place on the can.

2. Adhere one border sticker on top of the two papers and the second one at the bottom of the can.

3. Cut out a 4½" × 2¼" (4 × 6 cm) tag from the cream cardstock using the ruler, cutting mat, and craft knife. Embellish the tag with a small piece of the gingham border sticker, the rose bubblet sticker, and a pink bow.

4. Glue the tag and the rose to the can with a hot glue gun.

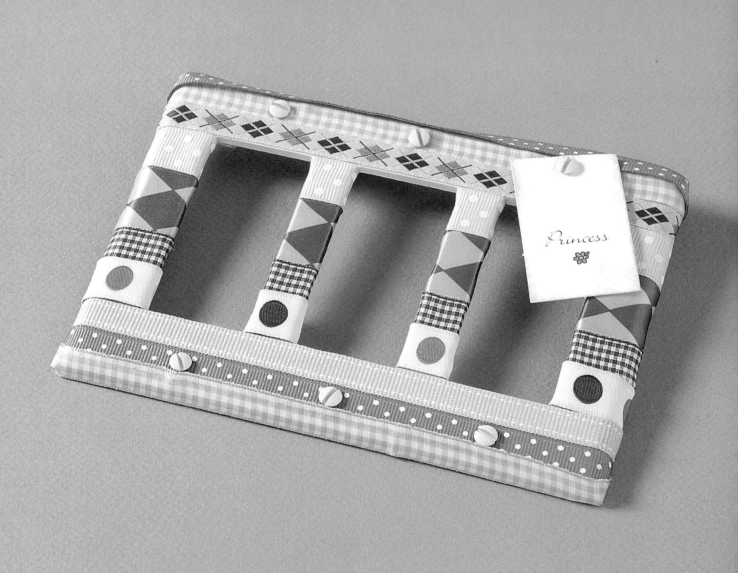

Princess **Light Switch Cover**

Designer: Michelle Hill

MATERIALS

- blank light switch cover
- ribbon
- "princess" tag

TOOLS

- cutting mat and craft knife
- tacky tape
- awl

This is such a fun and simple project to use up scraps of ribbon, trim, or fiber. You can also adhere rub-ons to the ribbon for a more personalized look.

1. Cover the entire surface of the switch plate with tacky tape.

2. Apply the ribbons horizontally to the entire surface of the plate.

3. Turn the switch plate over so the back side is facing you. Using the craft knife, slice down the middle of each hole in the switch plate to create tabs to fold over to the back side.

4. With the light switch still turned over, apply tacky tape to the whole back side. Starting at the top, fold the cut ends of the ribbon over and adhere it to the tacky tap. Repeat the process until all the cut ends are adhered to the back of the plate.

5. Use an awl to poke holes through the ribbon where the screws will be placed. Attach the "princess" tag through one of the screw holes.

Fridge **Magnets** and **Gift Tin**

Designer: Pam Kopka

MATERIALS

- 2 ⅞" (7.5 cm) metal tin
- epoxy page pebbles and circles
- magnets (same size or slightly smaller than page pebbles)
- patterned paper
- silk flower
- ribbon
- miniature tag
- acrylic paint

TOOLS

- glue
- gesso
- sandpaper
- foam paintbrush

Fridge magnets are a quick and easy project that the whole family can enjoy. Making magnets can be as simple as gluing a magnet to a beautiful scrapbook plaque or silk flower or as intricate as printing and enhancing photos or images.

1. Lightly sand the outside of the tin, and then apply a basecoat of gesso using a foam paintbrush.

2. Paint the tin using the foam paintbrush and acrylic paint. Let dry completely.

3. Glue ribbon around the top edge of the tin cover.

4. Trace around the bottom of the tin to make a circle on the patterned paper. Cut out the circle, making it slightly smaller than the traced image to fit it in the bottom of the tin. Glue in place.

5. Finish the tin cover by gluing on a silk flower, a miniature tag, and a piece of folded ribbon.

6. To make the magnets, adhere the page pebble to the patterned paper. Trim off the excess, then glue to the magnet.

Other Assorted Magnets

- For a photo magnet: Attach a page pebble to a small photo, trim the excess, and mount on a magnet.
- For a flower magnet: Attach a silk flower to a magnet. Tie a tiny scrap of ribbon through a button and glue the button to the top of the silk flower.
- For epoxy embellishment magnets: Attach assorted epoxy embellishments to magnets.
- For a bottle cap magnet: Attach a bottle cap to a magnet. Embellish the inside of the bottle cap using a page pebble over an image, an epoxy embellishment, or other circular items.

Paper-Wrapped **Candles** and Matching **Tray**

Designer: Michelle Hill

For the Candles

MATERIALS

- one 5" (13 cm) pillar candle
- two 3" (7.5 cm) pillar candles
- assorted 12" × 12" (30.5 × 30.5 cm) sheets of patterned paper
- ⅛" (0.3 cm) acid-free double-sided tape
- silk flowers
- ribbon
- wooden beads
- seed beads

TOOLS

- cutting mat and craft knife
- scissors
- ruler

For the Matching Tray

MATERIALS

- 4" × 10" (10 × 25.5 cm) photo frame
- assorted 12" × 12" (30.5 × 30.5 cm) sheets of patterned paper
- ⅛" (0.3 cm) acid-free double-sided tape
- silk flowers
- ribbon
- seed beads

TOOLS

- cutting mat and craft knife
- glue
- scissors

This tray makes a beautiful sideboard decoration with the matching candles, or it can be used alone on a dresser to hold perfume bottles, jewelry, or other precious items.

For the Large Candle

1. Cut a piece of the patterned paper measuring 11" × 4" (28 × 10 cm) using the ruler, cutting mat, and craft knife. Wrap the patterned paper around the candle and secure with double-sided tape.

2. Trim the ribbon to fit around the candle, then adhere it in place on top of the patterned paper using double-sided tape. Attach three flowers to the front of the candle and embellish with the wooden beads.

For the Small Candles

1. Cut two pieces of patterned paper measuring 6½" × 2" (16.5 × 5 cm) using the ruler, cutting mat, and craft knife. Wrap the patterned paper strips around the two smaller candles, one at a time, and secure with double-sided tape.

2. Trim ribbon to fit around each candle, then adhere it on the top of the patterned paper using double-sided tape. Attach one flower to the front of each candle and then add the seed bead in the center.

For the Matching Tray

1. Cut a piece of the patterned paper measuring 4" × 10" (10 × 25.5 cm) using the ruler, cutting mat, and craft knife. Place the paper beneath the glass of the frame.

2. Measure and cut the patterned paper pieces to fit the frame using the ruler, cutting mat, and craft knife. Adhere the patterned paper to the front of the frame, then wrap the excess around to the back of the frame. Secure the papers in place using double-sided tape.

3. Measure and cut sections of ribbon for each side, then adhere. Add three flowers and seed beads on each side. Add additional ribbon to the corners of the tray.

Altered **Child's Puzzle**

Designer: Lori Roberts

MATERIALS

- black-and-white photos
- child's cardboard puzzle with large pieces
- patterned paper
- alphabet patterned paper
- yellow cardstock
- ribbon
- blue staples
- letter and number beads
- caption sticker
- clear word sticker
- black alphabet stickers
- acrylic paint

TOOLS

- cutting mat and craft knife
- paper adhesive
- glossy gel medium
- glossy accents medium
- awl
- small hammer
- stapler
- fine sandpaper
- large stiff brush (for dry brushing)
- foam paintbrush

For this project a 9" × 11⅜" (23 × 29 cm) child's cardboard puzzle was taken apart, altered, and then put back together. The collage on top honors a young boy's first haircut, but you could alter the theme to celebrate any accomplishment.

1. Remove the puzzle pieces from the puzzle. Paint the puzzle "frame" using the acrylic paint. Start with the lightest colors first, then move on to the darker colors. Let the frame dry completely.

2. Using the paper adhesive, cover the puzzle pieces with the patterned paper. Let the puzzle pieces dry completely, then trim off the excess using the craft knife. Sand the edges of the puzzle pieces so they will fit back into the puzzle frame.

3. Apply the paper adhesive to the puzzle frame and glue in the altered puzzle pieces. Let dry completely. Dry-brush paint onto the puzzle to give a distressed look, then sand lightly. Let dry completely. Apply glossy gel medium to the entire surface to seal.

4. Adhere the photos to the cardstock, trim the edges, and glue to the board using the glossy accents medium.

5. Trim the larger photo and apply a clear word sticker ("cherish"), then adhere the photo in place using the glossy accents.

6. Attach ribbons to the left-hand side of the collage with a stapler and the colored staples. Glue the alphabet tiles, beads, and buttons in place as desired using the glossy accents medium.

7. Using the small hammer and the awl, punch holes at the top of the puzzle and string ribbons through for hanging.

Spring **Door Wreath**

Designer: Michelle Hill

MATERIALS

- 14" (35.5 cm) straw craft wreath
- pink spray paint
- assorted patterned paper
- buttons
- silk flowers
- rhinestone brads
- chipboard letters to spell "spring"
- ribbon
- rub-ons
- floss

TOOLS

- glue dots
- glossy accents medium
- sewing needle
- flower die
- ⅛" (0.3 cm) hole punch
- foam paintbrush
- pencil

Once complete, you can hang this spring wreath on your door or just about anywhere in your house. This project can be altered to make any themed wreath using holiday scrap papers.

1. Working in a well-ventilated area, spray paint the wreath using the pink spray paint. Let the wreath dry completely.

2. Using the flower die, cut out various sizes of flowers from the patterned papers. Using a foam paintbrush, apply glossy accents over the cutouts and let them dry.

3. Hand-sew the buttons to the center of the paper flowers using the needle and the floss.

4. Line up the monogram chipboard letters to spell the word "spring." Use a pencil to mark a dot where your holes will go to tie the letters together using assorted ribbons. Punch the holes using the hole punch. Tie the letters together. Add the rub-on word "blossom" to the letter "R."

5. Punch a hole at the top of the "S" and the "G," then tie the word "spring" to the wreath using ribbon.

6. Attach the paper flowers to the wreath using glue dots. Adhere the silk flowers to the wreath by pushing rhinestone brads through the middle of each flower.

Cigar Box **Purse**

Designer: Kim Pennington

MATERIALS

- cigar box
- patterned paper
- black glossy acrylic paint
- monogram letter "B"
- seven pink sequins
- beads for handle
- metal handle and hinges

TOOLS

- cutting mat and craft knife
- clear acrylic spray (e.g., Krylon)
- 2" (5 cm) paintbrush
- brayer
- water-based sealer (e.g., Mod Podge)
- crystal clear top coat satin oil-based sealer (e.g., Krylon)
- screwdriver
- toothpicks

You can create a unique and special gift—or a purse to use for yourself—using an old cigar box. For this purse the designer worked backwards from the paper she selected but there are hundreds of possibilities for turning used boxes into functional art.

1. Paint the entire box using the black acrylic paint. Let the box dry completely, and then repeat for the second coat. Let the box dry overnight.

2. Using the ruler, cutting mat, and craft knife, cut out pieces of paper to fit along the front, sides, back, and inside of the purse.

3. Spray the paper pieces and the letter monogram with the clear acrylic spray, then let dry at least one hour (or following the manufacturer's instructions).

4. Adhere the paper and the monogram to the box using the water-based sealer. Smooth the pieces using the brayer to eliminate air bubbles. Let the box dry completely.

5. Coat the entire purse with crystal clear top coat satin oil-based sealer.

6. Add the pink sequins using a toothpick and glue. Add beads to the handle, and then attach the handle using the screwdriver.

CONTRIBUTORS

Christine Adolph
info@christineadolph.com
www.christineadolph.com
Christine has been a designer for more than ten years, and she is constantly drawn to floral collage, surface pattern design, and illustration. She holds a BFA from Otis College of Art and Design and an MFA from the Rhode Island School of Design. She lives just a few steps from the ocean in San Clemente, California, with her husband and two girls.

Carla Asmus
carla.asmus@gmail.com
For the past few years Carla has been one of the designers for Frances Meyer. Working and teaching in this industry has been a dream come true for Carla. She relishes every opportunity to share her enthusiasm and creativity with others. When she is not paper crafting, she can be found horseback riding, painting, or browsing at the local bookstore.

Jenna Beegle
Although Jenna started her design career using a needle and thread, she also loves the art of paper crafting. Her work has appeared in *Memory Makers, Legacy, Somerset Studio,* and *Paper Crafts* magazines.

Linda Blinn
ljblinn@pacbell.net
Linda participates in the world of mixed-media art as an author, teacher, designer, and artist. Her art has appeared in numerous magazines, including *Victoria* and *Cloth Paper Scissors.* Her first book, *Making Family Journals,* will be available in spring 2006. She lives in the small coastal town of San Clemente, California, with her husband, Tom.

Sue Campbell
scampbell@faithworksart.com
www.faithworksart.com
Sue is an artist, writer, and burgeoning voice for the Divine Feminine who has created a vehicle for self-expression in her business, Faithworksart. She lives in Andover, Massachusetts, with her husband, Jeff, and since the nest was emptied several years ago, she has filled it again with two dogs and a cat. Her main passion is writing, but she also uses watercolors as a backdrop to her inspirational prose.

Amber Crosby
ambercrosby@hotmail.com
Amber is a native Texan with a Bachelor of Arts in English Literature. Scrapbooking combines her love for paper crafts with her passion for photography. She is a stay-at-home mom to her son, Collin, who stars in most of her layouts. Amber was chosen as a 2005 Paperkuts Power Team member and has been published in *Creating Keepsakes; Simple Scrapbooks; Paper Crafts; Stamp It!; Scrapbooks, Etc.; Ivy Cottage;* and *Memory Makers* magazines.

Deborah Fay D'Onofrio
donofdsn@comcast.net
Art and healing are inextricably linked in Deborah's work. She is a mixed-media artist with interests including collage, photography, altered books, oracles, journals, and ritual tools. She is the founder of Earth Meets Sky, a line of inspirational greeting cards. As a Reiki Master, intuitive, workshop facilitator, and ritual leader, she melds creativity as a therapeutic metaphor. Deborah lives in Massachusetts with her husband and son, both resident muses.

Holly Sar Dye
hsd@bufobufo.com
An elementary school teacher by weekday, Holly enjoys bookmaking, paper arts, and rubber-stamping in her free time. She shares her passion for art with her students and friends. Holly lives in California with her husband, Philip, and her son, Alec. Her work has previously been published in *Time* magazine and *Pockets, Pullouts, and Hiding Places: Interactive Elements for Altered Books, Memory Art, and Collage.*

Kitty Foster
kfost108@bellsouth.net
Kitty started scrapbooking several years ago and hasn't stopped since. She teaches scrapbooking at retreats and conventions and has been published in several magazines, including *Memory Makers* and *Scrapbooks, Etc.* She has a loving husband, three boys, and a princess. In her free time she enjoys reading, photography, and church activities.

Suzee Gallagher
Suzee.Gallagher@yahoo.com
Suzee is the consulting scrapbook editor for *Legacy* magazine and is active in many aspects of the scrapbook industry, including having her own line of scrapbook papers and embellishments. Suzee is known for her innovative techniques and advocates experimenting with us materials—any materials! She is also an acc plished photographer. She lives in Villa Park, California, with her husband and two childre

Lisa Grunewald
llgrunewald@hotmail.com
Lisa and her husband, Mick, live outside Columbus, Ohio. After teaching elementary school for ten years, Lisa recently put her ca on hold to stay at home with her son, Nate, and daughter, Grace. Lisa is an independer consultant who has worked with Elmer's Products to develop their Storykeepers line o scrapbooking tools. She also teaches scrapbooking classes and enjoys travel, photogra and cooking.

Michelle Hill
croppin@adelphia.net
Michelle is a published designer and curren a creative designer for Li'l Davis Designs. Sh also teaches locally and nationally. Michelle resides in Carlsbad, California, with her hus band, Evan, and their four children, Danika, Caitlin, Lillie, and Seth. When not serving a Mom taxi, she can be found preparing clas kits or organizing her ever growing scrap space.

Pam Kopka
pamkopka@comcast.net
Pam is a kindergarten teacher who lives in the tiny town of New Galilee, Pennsylvania, with her husband, Denny, and her two daughters. Pam's love of art started at a you age, and she has been scrapbooking for twelve years. She was chosen for the Hall o Fame in 2003 and her work has been published industry wide.

Jenn Mason
jenn@jennmason.com
www.JennMason.com
Jenn is a paper and mixed-media artist. She is the author of *Pockets, Pullouts, and Hiding Places* and is writing an exciting new paper book series. Jenn teaches internationally and recently moved to Boston, Massachusetts.

Stephanie McAtee
Stephanie lives in Kansas City, Missouri, and has been scrapbooking since 2000. She ha always had a passion for journaling and pho raphy and enjoys using dimensional, interac elements in her art. Her main focus when sh

king is the hope that one day her boys, ...y and Ethan, will sit down with her jour-... and know both what she was thinking and ...ng and the depth that she put into her art ...their lives.

...dy Morris

...dy has been scrapbooking for more than ...n years and enjoys thinking outside the ... She teaches scrapbooking and stamping ...has served on several different design ...ns. In addition to scrapbooking, Wendy ...ys drawing portraits and still-life settings, ...eling, her ministry, spending time with family, ...reading. She lives in the small town of ...selle, Alabama.

...Pennington

...nie_pennington@yahoo.com ...has always found herself dipping into ...s and paints express herself. She loves ...ing cigar-box purses and other projects, ...ch she says come from the windows ...er soul.

...Roberts

...was born and raised in western New York, ...re summers can be very hot and the winters ...very cold and long. She serves on several ...gn teams, including Unmounted Central, ...r Studiowerx, Buzz and Bloom, Hearts ...ouch, and The Paper Artist Place. She espe-...y enjoys combining scrapbook supplies ...rubber stamps.

...by Schuh

...by lives near Buffalo, New York, and is a ...designer for Anna Griffin, Inc. She teaches ...crapbooking events across the country and ...s creating projects with beautiful papers.

...a Smith

...a teaches book art and heritage classes at ...apdoodles near her home in Fredericksburg, ...inia. She is a design-team member for ...sor Sisters. She lives with her husband of ...nty-two years (not to mention best friend), ...y, and her teenage daughter, Jordan.

...nine Stein

...nelson@yahoo.com ...nine has been involved with book and ...er arts for more than a decade. In addition ...eaching, her work has appeared in numer-...scrapbook and stamping magazines.

Allison Strine

allisonstrine@mac.com

Allison is a mixed-media artist who loves to play with paper, paints, fabrics, and polymer clay. Her work has appeared in *Somerset Studio*, *Legacy*, *Cloth Paper Scissors*, and several other scrapbook magazines. Allison's projects are featured in the books *Your Sentiments Exactly* (Creative Imaginations) and *Pockets, Pullouts, and Hiding Places* by Jenn Mason. She lives in Atlanta, Georgia, with her right-brained husband and two children.

Sarah Tyler

sarah@youngtylers.com

Sarah began scrapbooking in 2000 but altered art was a recent and thrilling discovery for her. Sarah is a senior product review writer at ScrapFriends.com and a designer for Scissor Sisters. Her work has appeared in Quarry Books, Pinecone Press, and Cantata Books idea books and publications. Sarah makes her home in Indiana with her husband and two young sons.

Sandy Wisneski

Sandy lives in Ripon, Wisconsin, and has been stamping for fourteen years. Her work has been published in *The Rubberstamper*, *Vamp Stamp News*, and *CorrespondenceArt*. She has designed for a variety of companies including Stamp Francisco and Art by Moonlight. By day she is a reading specialist at Ripon Middle School.

SUPPLY CONTRIBUTORS

Special thanks to the following manufacturers for contributing their products for use in this book or assisting with individual projects.

Anna Griffin, Inc.

733 Lambert Drive
Atlanta, GA 30324
888.817.8170
info@annagriffin.com
www.annagriffin.com
Papers, frames, and albums for the scrapbook market. Also offers a large collection of stationery and gift items, including notecards, notepads, greeting cards, file folders, office pads, and letterhead.

Lazar Studiowerx, Inc.

P.O. Box 1489
Point Roberts, WA 98281-1489
866.478.9379
info@lazarstudiowerx.com
www.lazarstudiowerx.com
Limited edition and other decorative papers and matching die-cut embellishments, rubons, fiber packs, and rubber stamps.

Making Memories

1168 West 500 North
Centerville, UT 84014
801.294.0430
www.makingmemories.com
Offers more than 4,500 different products for scrapbookers, including charms, labels, brads, eyelets, fibers, hinges, metal words, page pebbles, snaps, and tags.

Scissor Sisters, Inc.

267 B East 29th Street
Suite 265
Loveland, CO 80538
877.773.7780
info@scissor-sisters.com
www.scissor-sisters.com
Wide assortment of decorative patterned paper and matching stickers, as well as cards, projects, albums, and scrapbook layouts.

PRODUCT MANUFACTURERS BY PROJECT

To help you locate manufacturers for the supplies used in making the projects for this book, each project is listed here by page number. For more information about a specific manufacturer, see Resources, page 124.

Attitude Is Everything Card, 12
Marigold cardstock (Bazzill Basics); Colormates Light Racy Raspberry cardstock (WorldWin); Fresh! paperWERX collection Pink Sidewalk Chalk patterned paper (Lazar Studiowerx); "Attitude is Everything" Soft Spoken Embellishment (Me & My Big Idea); silk flowers (Prima); ribbon (American Crafts)

Critter Gift Cards and Tags, 14
Textured purple gift card (Design with a View); decorative brad (Making Memories); light blue textured gift card (Design with a View); Paper Edge Ripple scissors (Fiskars); chalked-look dark blue gift tag (Paperbilities); chalked-look light blue gift tag (Paperbilities); P-06 Texture Cream decorative paper (Scissor Sisters)

I Love You Card, 16
5306-203 Beaucoup de Chocolate patterned paper (Frances Meyer); 5306-202 Box of Chocolates patterned paper (Frances Meyer); 5306-199 Raspberry Sorbet patterned paper (Frances Meyer); BBLT-104 Hearts Bubblet sticker (Frances Meyer)

Candy Wrapper Variation, 16
Decorative papers and bubblet stickers (Frances Meyer).

Dragonfly Celebrate Card, 19
Cool Metallics Arctic Snow frosted white paper (The Paper Company); Decorative Elements dragonfly (The Card Connection); Fun Fibers for Fabulous Effects (EK Success)

Celebrate Wedding Card, 21
Cardstock (Bazzill Basics); Over The Moon Press Embossed patterned paper (EK Success); vellum paper (Bazzill Basics); Architexture Building Embellishments metal sticker (EK Success); eyelet word (Making Memories); mini-brads (Making Memories); Edwardian Script Font

Japanese Collage Card, 22
Half-fold greeting cards #3297 (Avery); bold blue cardstock (The Paper Company); textured yellow paper (Funky Textures); green craft paper #42-5157 (Provo); Fun Fibers for Fabulous Effects (EK Success)

Wedding Gift Card Enclosure, 24
Lasting Impressions textured cardstock (Paper Inc.); SLW09 The Best of Friends sticky words (All My Memories); The WoodStone Collection Wedding photo banner stickers #09203 (Cloud Design); Jolee's Boutique Jolee's By You wedding embellishments (EK Success)

Thank-You Card, 27
5306-172 Blue Damask patterned paper (Francis Meyer); 5306-178 English Ivy patterned paper (Frances Meyer); 2170-207 Hydrangea Memories border sticker (Frances Meyer); 2170-208 Flowers and gingham border sticker (Frances Meyer); BBLT-102 Hydrangea Garden Bubblet Sticker (Frances Meyer); 5157-119 Sour Apple Textured Cardstock (Frances Meyer)

Paper Tissue Flower Card, 28
Matte-coated notecards (Staples); textured green paper (Funky Textures)

I Miss You Card, 30
Bahama cardstock (Bazzill Basics); Fresh! PaperWERX collection Grass Stains and Dazed and Confused patterned paper (Lazar Studiowerx); Fresh! PaperWERX collection tag (Lazar Studiowerx); fabric letter (Making Memories); silk flowers (Prima); alphabet stamps (PSX Design); gingham ribbon (Offray); teal mini-brad (Doodlebug Designs); "You" rub-on word (Creative Imaginations); square punch (Marvy Uchida)

Best Wishes Wedding Card, 33
AG2002 Vellum (Anna Griffin); AG102 Rosebud patterned paper (Anna Griffin); rose and flower AG557 die cut (Anna Griffin); AG642 border sticker (Anna Griffin)

Imagine Greeting Card, 35
Big Kahuna patterned paper (Lazar Studiowerx) ; Elements Tintype letters (Lazar Studiowerx)

Bamboo Greeting Card, 36
Bamboo stickers (Mrs. Grossman's)

Transparency Tulips Greeting Card, 3[
Rubberstamp: B021J Tulips rubber stam (Lazar Studiowerx); Big Kahuna pattern paper (Lazar Studiowerx); ink pad (Sta On)

Altered Composition Notebooks, 42
Fresh Papers, PW203 FRESH! Pink die-Tag and PW406 Island Girl fiberWERX (Lazar Studiowerx); "play" stamp (Artby Moonlight.com); Fresh Papers, PW20 FRESH! Chartreuse die-cut Tags and PW404 FRESH! Chartreuse fiberWERX (Lazar Studiowerx)

Be Embellished Journal, 45
Spiral-bound journal (Gallison); slide mo (Design Originals); patterned paper (Lollipop Shoppe); lowercase alphabet stamps (Alphabet Pixie); Asian stamp (A Impressions); garden nymph stamp (Michael's Crafts); gold metallic acrylic paint (Americana); pearl turquoise Lumie paint (Jacquard); white stencil paint (Plai

Reach Within Decorated Journal, 47
Bound journal (Fiorentina); white cardsto (Stampin' Up!); shrink plastic (Grafix; lo ercase alphabet stamps (Alphabet Pixie) Asian stamp (Art Impressions); Script star (Stampin' Up!)

Gift Tag Bag, 48
Single fold tags (Gartner Studios); foam flower stamp (Making Memories); ribbo (May Arts); beads (Westrim Crafts & Beads)

Gerber Daisy Coasters, 93
Rub-ons (Making Memories); Gerber daisy clip art; Mod Podge water-based sealer (Plaid)

Little Boy Frame, 95
Decorative patterned paper (David Walker, Creative Imaginations); rubber stamps (Technique Tuesday); stamp ink (Ranger); water-soluble markers (Tombow); vintage motorcycle toy purchased on www.ebay.com; gel medium (Golden)

Garden Votive Candleholder, 96
Jolee's Boutique Jolee's By you white fence, gardening can, dahlia, grass, and primrose flowers (EK Success)

Altered Child's Tin, 98
Metal tin (Target); Hot Pink Short Cuts and Mimosa Satin Home Décor spray paint (Krylon); Green Short Cuts Paint pen (Krylon); ribbon (SEI, www.FBTY.com, May Arts); Ice Cream Parlor patterned paper and stickers (Fancy Pants Designs); vintage photo ink (Ranger)

Seaside Altered CD, 101
Fun at the Beach stickers (Scissor Sisters); Buggy Blue and Sky Blue Plaid decorative paper (Scissor Sisters); Glossy Accents Dimensional Adhesive (Ranger); blue organza ribbon (Fibers By The Yard); Hammered Finish Spray Paint "Gold" (Rust-Oleum); Mod Podge "Gloss" (Plaid)

Dela Tribute Frame, 102
Patterned paper (Scissor Sisters); bubble-type alphabet letters (Li'l Davis); metal plaque (Making Memories)

Altered "C" Letter, 105
Patterned paper (Scissor Sisters); brads (Accent Depot); ribbon (Close to My Heart, Offray); acrylic paint (Plaid); Blackjack font

Altered Gift Can, 106
5306-170 Wild Rose Paper, 5306-169 English Rose Paper, 2170-206 Flowers & Gingham Border Sticker, BBLT-101 Rose Bubblet Sticker (Frances Meyer)

Princess Light Switch Cover, 109
Ribbon (Li'l Davis, May Arts); Princess tag (Making Memories)

Fridge Magnets and Gift Tin, 111
Sisters metal plaque (Making Memories); silk flower (Prima)

Paper-Wrapped Candles and Matching Tray, 112
Fresh! Collection (Warm and Fuzzy and Pink Sidewalk Chalk) patterned paper (Lazar Studiowerx); Big Kahuna Collection patterned paper (Lazar Studiowerx); SuperTape acid-free double-sided adhesive tape (Therm O Web); silk flowers (Prima); ribbon (American Crafts)

Altered Child's Puzzle, 114
Perfect Paper Adhesive (USArt Quest); glossy gel medium (Liquitex); Mini Stack Pad patterned paper (Die Cuts with a View); ribbon (May Arts); letter and number beads (The Beadery); caption sticker (Stickopotamus); alphabet patterned paper (7 Gypsies); clear word sticker (EK Success); black alphabet stickers (Frances Meyer); Glossy Accents (Ranger); True Teal and Light Blue acrylic paint (Plaid); glaze (Vernis Barniz)

Spring Door Wreath, 116
Tea Rose spray paint (Krylon); patterned paper (KI Memories); buttons (Hill Creek, DCWV); brads (SEI); chipboard letters (Li'l Davis); ribbon (May Arts); rub-ons (Making Memories); floss (DMC); Glossy Accents (Ranger); flower die (Sizzix)

Cigar Box Purse, 119
Patterned paper (Lollipop Shoppe); black gloss acrylic paint (Plaid's Apple Barrel brand)

RESOURCES

7 Gypsies
www.7gypsies.com
Scrapbook paper and embellishments

Accent Depot
www.accentdepot.com
Brads and other embellishments

Accucut
www.accucut.com
Die-cutting system, dies, and tools

AC Moore
www.acmoore.com
Art and craft supplies

Arizona Art Supply
www.arizonaartsupply.com
Art supplies

ArtCity
www.artcity.com
Art and craft supplies, frames, and furnitu

All My Memories
www.allmymemories.com
Paper, ribbon, and other scrapbook supp

American Crafts
www.americancrafts.com
Paper, vellum, embellishments, pens, mar and cards

Anna Griffin, Inc.
www.annagriffin.com
Decorative paper and embellishments

Ariden Creations
www.aridencreations.com
Wood embellishments

ArtChix
www.artchixstudio.com
Vintage images, rubber stamps, transpare cies, paper, and embellishments

Art Impressions
www.artimpressions.com
Rubber stamps

Autumn Leaves
www.autumnleaves.com
Scrapbook paper, books, and embellishm

Avery
www.avery.com
Office tags and supplies

BasicGrey
www.basicgrey.com
Cutting-edge decorative papers

Bazzill
www.bazzillbasics.com
Cardstock

y Patch
.bearypatchinc.com
r, stickers, and embellishments

y's Scrapbooks
.beckysscrapbooks.com
book supplies

Franklin Crafts
.bfranklincrafts.com
and scrapbook supplies

Kept Memories
.bestkeptmemories.com
book and paper-craft supplies

unny Press
.bobunny.com
lesale only—paper, stickers, and
uts

r Scrapbooks
.boxerscrapbooks.com
n, embellishments, paper, and stickers

d + D/termined
.bound-determined.com
ns and scrapbooks

ured Elements
.capturedelements.com
rative papers

lee's Creations
.carolees.com
rative paper and embellishments

terbox
.chatterboxinc.com
book paper and embellishments

rsnap
.clearsnap.com
er stamps and stamping ink

e to My Heart
.closetomyheart.com
ns, paper, ink, and kits

d 9
.cloud9design.com
er of Halo eyelet snaps

tive Design Boutique
.creativedesignboutique.com
book supplies, paper, and albums

Creative Imagination
www.cigift.com
Decorative paper, supplies, and
embellishments

Daisy Ds
www.daisydspaper.com
Decorative paper

Darby
www.darbypaper.com
Decorative paper and die cuts

Dena Designs
www.denadesigns.com
Embellishments, stickers, and paper

Delta
www.deltacrafts.com
Acrylic paint and craft supplies

Deluxe Designs
www.deluxecuts.com
Decorative paper, supplies, and
embellishments

Design Originals
www.d-originals.com
Scrapbook paper, supplies, and
embellishments

Dick Blick Art materials
www.dickblick.com
Art supplies

Die Cuts with a View
www.dcwv.com
Mat, paper, and quote stacks, stickers,
rub-ons, albums, paper and cardstock,
and embellishments

Diane's Daughters
www.dianesdaughters.com
Themed papers, die cuts, tags, and
embellishments

DMC
www.dmc.com
Embroidery thread and other fibers

Doodlebug Designs
www.doodlebug.ws
Kits, papers, stickers, buttons, paper posies,
sequins, ribbon, and embellishments

Endless Memories
www.endlessmemoriesonline.com
Scrapbook and paper-craft supplies

EK Success
www.eksuccess.com
Patterned paper, supplies, and
embellishments

Fibers by the Yard
www.fbty.com
Fiber, twill, ribbon, and trim

Fiskars
www.fiskars.com
Scissors, deckle-edge scissors, and other
cutting tools

Folk Art
www.folkartenterprises.com
Decorative painting, scrapbook, and
stamping supplies

Fontwerks
www.fontwerks.com
Paper, ribbon, and rubber stamps

Francis Meyer
www.francesmeyer.com
Stickers, paper, bubblets, and rub-ons

Funky Fibers
www.funkyfibers.com
Wholesale only—fibers by the yard

Gartner Studios
www.gartnerstudios.com
High-quality stationery, invitations, and
greeting cards

Global Solutions
www.globalsolutionsonline.com
Stationery, paper, embellishments, impression
seals, and sealing wax

Gone Scrappin'
www.gonescrappin.com
Paper, stickers, and embellishments

Grafix
www.grafixarts.com
Plastic films and decorative products

Hero Arts
www.heroarts.com
Artstamps

Hobby Lobby
www.hobbylobby.com
Craft supplies

IKEA
www.ikea.com
Home goods, fabric, and furniture

Imagination Project
www.imaginationproject.com
Scrapbook papers and supplies

Jacquard
www.jacquardproducts.com
Paints and pearlescent powders

Jo-Ann Fabric & Crafts
www.joann.com
Fabric, scrapbook, and craft supplies

Judikins
www.judikins.com
Rubber stamps, supplies, and Diamond Glaze

Junkitz
www.junkitz.com
Paper, fibers, buttons, and embellishments

KI Memories
www.kimemories.com
Scrapbook paper, supplies, and embellishments

K&Company
www.kandcompany.com
Scrapbook paper, albums, and embellishments

Kreinik Manufacturing
www.kreinik.com
Threads, beads, and fiber

Krylon
www.krylon.com
Spray and brush-on paints and finishes

Lazar Studiowerx
www.lazarstudiowerx.com
Decorative papers, die cuts, rub-ons, fiber, and stamps

Lasting Impressions
www.lastingimpressions.com
Brass templates and embossing supplies

Li'l Davis
www.lildavisdesigns.com
Scrapbook paper, supplies, and embellishments

Liquitex
www.liquitex.com
Paint and craft finishes

Loersch Corp.
www.loersch.com
Slide mounts, frames, and tools

Magic Scraps
www.magicscraps.com
Scrapbook embellishments and supplies

Making Memories
www.makingmemories.com
Scrapbook paper, tools, supplies, and embellishments

Marvy Uchida
www.uchida.com
Markers, ink, and hole punches

May Arts
www.mayarts.com
Wholesale only—ribbon

Maya Road
www.mayaroad.com
Wholesale only—fiber, stickers, and embellishments

Me & My Big Ideas
www.meandmybigideas.com
Scrapbook paper, supplies, and embellishments

Melissa Frances
www.melissafrances.com
Labels, paper, frames, tags, and transfers

Memories Complete
www.memoriescomplete.com
Tags, cardstock, paper, stickers, and rub-ons

Mrs. Grossman's
www.mrsgrossmans.com
Stickers

Michael's
www.michaels.com
Art and craft supplies

National Cardstock
www.nationalcardstock.com
Wholesale only—papers and vellums

Oak Leaf Acre
www.oakleafacre.com
Scrapbook supplies

Office World
http://store.officeworld.com
Office supplies

Pearl Paint
www.pearlpaint.com
Art supplies

Offray
www.offray.com
Ribbon

Paper Addict
www.paperaddict.com
Scrapbook paper

Paper Style
www.paperstyle.com
Scrapbook supplies, invitations, and stationery

Peddler's Pack
www.peddlerspack.com
Rubber stamps

Plaid
www.plaidenterprises.com
Acrylic paint, stamps, paper, and tools

Pressed Petals
www.pressedpetals.com
Pressed flowers, stickers, paper, vellum, and tags

Prism
www.prismpapers.com
Fine cardstock

Pottery Barn
www.potterybarn.com
Furniture and accessories

Provo
www.provocraft.com
Wholesale only—cutting systems and too paper, stickers, embellishments, and albu

w.psxdesign.com
stamps and supplies

en & Co
w.queenandco.com
ets, glitter, beads, and embellishments

ckutz
w.quickutz.com
cutting machine, alphabet and shaped

ger
w.rangerink.com
ink pads, and related products

Shop
w.ragshop.com
t supplies, fabric, frames, and florals

Art
w.rexart.com
supplies

r City Rubber Works
w.rivercityrubberworks.com
ber stamps

ber Stampede
w.rubberstampede.com
ber stamps and art stamps

y Pickle
//homepage.mac.com/rustypickle
ms, hardware, ink, leather, lace, paper,
on, stamps, stickers, and tags

sor Sisters
w.scissorsisters.com
er, tags, and embellishments

pWorks
w.scrapworks.com
pbook paper, tools, supplies, and
ellishments

pbook Discounts Galore
w.scrapbookdiscountsgalore.com
pbook supplies

p Talk
w.scraptalk.com
pbook supplies and product reviews

Scraps Ahoy
www.scrapsahoy.com
Scrapbook community

Stampin' Up
www.stampinup.com
Home party art stamps

Staples
www.staples.com
Scrapbook papers and albums,
office supplies

Stickers Galore
www.stickersgalore.com
Stickers

Sunshine Discount Crafts
www.sunshinecrafts.com
Craft supplies

Target
www.target.com
Home accessories and stationery supplies

Therm O Web
www.thermoweb.com
Adhesives

Tomorrow's Memories
www.tomemories.com
Scrapbook supplies

Two Peas in a Bucket
www.twopeasinabucket.com
Scrapbook supplies, ideas, and community

Walnut Hollow
www.walnuthollow.com
Wood embellishments

Westrim
www.westrimcrafts.com
Scrapbook and paper-art embellishments

About the Author

Photo by Jeff Smith

Barbara Bourassa is a craft designer, photographer, writer, and editor living in North Andover, Massachusetts, She resides with her husband Marc, who builds boats and furniture, and her two sons, Alex and Jack, who are very creative in their own right.

Barbara has been involved with crafts since becoming a Girl Scout at age ten, when she quickly earned all the art- and nature-related badges. She is especially drawn to natural materials, animals, and nature themes, and finds inspiration among the flowers, woods, and water of the Adirondacks, the mountains of New Hampshire, and her own backyard.

Her professional credentials include writing and editing positions with several magazines, including *Handcraft Illustrated*, *Cook's Illustrated*, *Natural Health*, and *PC Week*. *Beyond Scrapbooks* is her first book with Quarry Books.

Acknowledgments

First and foremost I'd like to thank Mary Ann Hall, my editor at Rockport, for giving me the chance to write this book. There's a certain risk involved in signing any first-time author, and I appreciate her trust in me to transform a few thoughts and sentences into a 128-page published work of art.

I'd also like to thank my husband, Marc, and my two sons, Alex and Jack, for putting up with endless packages, bubble wrap, projects, paper scraps, and assorted scrapbooking do-dads all over my office for months on end. They are used to hearing the words, "Please don't touch that," and "Want to come to AC Moore with me?" and I love them for always responding positively.

Thank you to all the wonderful artists, crafters, and designers who contributed to this book. Each time I connected with one of you it was like finding a kindred creative spirit in a sea of chaos. Your energy, enthusiasm, and willingness to meet my deadlines were incredible, but the projects themselves are beyond beautiful. Thank you, one and all, for taking time from your busy lives to contribute to this book and to share your creative energy with me.

And thank you to all the support staff at Rockport who will help take this book from a manuscript and four boxes of projects to a finished book with beautiful photos, carefully edited directions, and lists of resources for supplies.

And last, but not least, thank you to my mom, who always encouraged me to be creative. There's a little part of you in every single thing I make, Ma.